MznLnx

Missing Links Exam Preps

Exam Prep for

Thinking Mathematically

Blitzer, 4th Edition

The MznLnx Exam Prep is your link from the texbook and lecture to your exams.
The MznLnx Exam Preps are unauthorized and comprehensive reviews of your textbooks.

All material provided by MznLnx and Rico Publications (c) 2010
Textbook publishers and textbook authors do not particpate in or contribute to these reviews.

MznLnx

Rico Publications

Exam Prep for Thinking Mathematically
4th Edition
Blitzer

Publisher: Raymond Houge
Assistant Editor: Michael Rouger
Text and Cover Designer: Lisa Buckner
Marketing Manager: Sara Swagger
Project Manager, Editorial Production: Jerry Emerson
Art Director: Vernon Lowerui

Product Manager: Dave Mason
Editorial Assitant: Rachel Guzmanji
Pedagogy: Debra Long
Cover Image: Jim Reed/Getty Images
Text and Cover Printer: City Printing, Inc.
Compositor: Media Mix, Inc.

(c) 2010 Rico Publications
ALL RIGHTS RESERVED. No part of this work covered by the copyright may be reproduced or used in any form or by an means--graphic, electronic, or mechanical, including photocopying, recording, taping, Web distribution, information storage, and retrieval systems, or in any other manner--without the written permission of the publisher.

Printed in the United States
ISBN:

For more information about our products, contact us at:
Dave.Mason@RicoPublications.com

For permission to use material from this text or product, submit a request online to:
Dave.Mason@RicoPublications.com

Contents

CHAPTER 1
Problem Solving and Critical Thinking — 1

CHAPTER 2
Set Theory — 10

CHAPTER 3
Logic — 16

CHAPTER 4
Number Representation and Calculation — 21

CHAPTER 5
Number Theory and the Real Number System — 26

CHAPTER 6
Algebra: Equations and Inequalities — 40

CHAPTER 7
Algebra: Graphs, Functions, and Linear Systems — 51

CHAPTER 8
Consumer Mathematics and Financial Management — 63

CHAPTER 9
Measurement — 69

CHAPTER 10
Geometry — 73

CHAPTER 11
Counting Methods and Probability Theory — 94

CHAPTER 12
Statistics — 102

CHAPTER 13
Mathematical Systems — 113

CHAPTER 14
Voting and Apportionment — 120

CHAPTER 15
Graph Theory — 122

ANSWER KEY — 127

TO THE STUDENT

COMPREHENSIVE

The *MznLnx* Exam Prep series is designed to help you pass your exams. Editors at MznLnx review your textbooks and then prepare these practice exams to help you master the textbook material. Unlike study guides, workbooks, and practice tests provided by the texbook publisher and textbook authors, *MznLnx* gives you **all** of the material in each chapter in exam form, not just samples, so you can be sure to nail your exam.

MECHANICAL

The MznLnx Exam Prep series creates exams that will help you learn the subject matter as well as test you on your understanding. Each question is designed to help you master the concept. Just working through the exams, you gain an understanding of the subject--its a simple mechanical process that produces success.

INTEGRATED STUDY GUIDE AND REVIEW

MznLnx is not just a set of exams designed to test you, its also a comprehensive review of the subject content. Each exam question is also a review of the concept, making sure that you will get the answer correct without having to go to other sources of material. You learn as you go! Its the easiest way to pass an exam.

HUMOR

Studying can be tedious and dry. MznLnx's instructional design includes moderate humor within the exam questions on occassion, to break the tedium and revitalize the brain

Chapter 1. Problem Solving and Critical Thinking

1. _____ consists of mental processes of discernment, analysis and evaluation. It includes possible processes of reflecting upon a tangible or intangible item in order to form a solid judgment that reconciles scientific evidence with common sense. In contemporary usage 'critical' has a certain negative connotation that does not apply in the present case.
   - a. Parametric operator
   - b. Critical thinking
   - c. Counterpart theory
   - d. Finite model property

2. In mathematics, a _____ is a polynomial equation of the second degree. The general form is

$$ax^2 + bx + c = 0,$$

   where a ≠ 0.

   The letters a, b, and c are called coefficients: the quadratic coefficient a is the coefficient of x^2, the linear coefficient b is the coefficient of x, and c is the constant coefficient, also called the free term or constant term.

   - a. Quartic equation
   - b. Quadratic equation
   - c. Linear equation
   - d. Difference of two squares

3. In mathematics, a _____ is a constant multiplicative factor of a certain object. For example, in the expression $9x^2$, the _____ of x^2 is 9.

   The object can be such things as a variable, a vector, a function, etc.

   - a. Stability radius
   - b. Fibonacci polynomials
   - c. Multivariate division algorithm
   - d. Coefficient

4. _____ is the study of the principles of valid demonstration and inference. _____ is a branch of philosophy, a part of the classical trivium of grammar, _____, and rhetoric. of λογικΐŒς, 'possessed of reason, intellectual, dialectical, argumentative', from λΐŒγος logos, 'word, thought, idea, argument, account, reason, or principle'.
   - a. Counterpart theory
   - b. Satisfiability
   - c. Boolean function
   - d. Logic

5. _____ is the likelihood or chance that something is the case or will happen. Theoretical _____ is used extensively in areas such as statistics, mathematics, science and philosophy to draw conclusions about the likelihood of potential events and the underlying mechanics of complex systems.

   The word _____ does not have a consistent direct definition.

   - a. Statistical significance
   - b. Probability
   - c. Standardized moment
   - d. Discrete random variable

6. _____ is the branch of mathematics concerned with analysis of random phenomena. The central objects of _____ are random variables, stochastic processes, and events: mathematical abstractions of non-deterministic events or measured quantities that may either be single occurrences or evolve over time in an apparently random fashion. Although an individual coin toss or the roll of a die is a random event, if repeated many times the sequence of random events will exhibit certain statistical patterns, which can be studied and predicted.

a. Standard probability space
b. Law of large numbers
c. Probability theory
d. Martingale central limit theorem

7. A _____ is the result of applying a function to a set of data.

More formally, statistical theory defines a _____ as a function of a sample where the function itself is independent of the sample's distribution: the term is used both for the function and for the value of the function on a given sample.

A _____ is distinct from an unknown statistical parameter, which is not computable from a sample.

a. Statistic
b. Spatial dependence
c. Parameter space
d. Loss function

8. _____ is a mathematical science pertaining to the collection, analysis, interpretation or explanation, and presentation of data. It also provides tools for prediction and forecasting based on data. It is applicable to a wide variety of academic disciplines, from the natural and social sciences to the humanities, government and business.

a. Percentile rank
b. Probability distribution
c. Regression toward the mean
d. Statistics

9. _____ is that which is owed; usually referencing assets owed, but the term can cover other obligations. In the case of assets, _____ is a means of using future purchasing power in the present before a summation has been earned.

a. Cobb-Douglas
b. Point-slope form
c. Metaheuristic
d. Debt

10. In mathematics, _____ and undefined are used to explain whether or not expressions have meaningful, sensible, and unambiguous values. Not all branches of mathematics come to the same conclusion.

The following expressions are undefined in all contexts, but remarks in the analysis section may apply.

a. Plugging in
b. Defined
c. LHS
d. Toy model

11. The word _____ has many distinct meanings in different fields of knowledge, depending on their methodologies and the context of discussion. Broadly speaking we can say that a _____ is some kind of belief or claim that (supposedly) explains, asserts, or consolidates some class of claims. Additionally, in contrast with a theorem the statement of the _____ is generally accepted only in some tentative fashion as opposed to regarding it as having been conclusively established.

a. Per mil
b. Transport of structure
c. Defined
d. Theory

12. In mathematics, a _____ is a mathematical statement which appears resourceful, but has not been formally proven to be true under the rules of mathematical logic. Once a _____ is formally proven true it is elevated to the status of theorem and may be used afterwards without risk in the construction of other formal mathematical proofs. Until that time, mathematicians may use the _____ on a provisional basis, but any resulting work is itself provisional until the underlying _____ is cleared up.

a. Moral certainty
b. Whitehead conjecture
c. Heawood conjecture
d. Conjecture

13. A hypothesis consists either of a suggested explanation for an observable phenomenon or of a reasoned proposal predicting a possible causal correlation among multiple phenomena. The term derives from the Greek, hypotithenai meaning 'to put under' or 'to suppose.' The scientific method requires that one can test a scientific hypothesis. Scientists generally base such _____ on previous observations or on extensions of scientific theories.
   a. 120-cell
   b. 2-3 heap
   c. 1-center problem
   d. Hypotheses

14. Induction or _____, sometimes called inductive logic, is the process of reasoning in which the premises of an argument are believed to support the conclusion but do not entail it;. Induction is a form of reasoning that makes generalizations based on individual instances. It is used to ascribe properties or relations to types based on an observation instance; or to formulate laws based on limited observations of recurring phenomenal patterns.
   a. Idempotency of entailment
   b. Inductive reasoning
   c. Intuitionistic logic
   d. Affine logic

15. _____ is the noteworthy alignment of two or more events or circumstances without obvious causal connection. The word is derived from the Latin co- and incidere.

The index of _____ can be used to analyze whether two events are related.

   a. 120-cell
   b. 1-center problem
   c. 2-3 heap
   d. Coincidence

16. Leonardo of Pisa (c. 1170 - c. 1250), also known as Leonardo Pisano, Leonardo Bonacci, Leonardo _____, or, most commonly, simply _____, was an Italian mathematician, considered by some 'the most talented mathematician of the Middle Ages'.
   a. Guido Castelnuovo
   b. Ralph C. Merkle
   c. Harry Hinsley
   d. Fibonacci

17. In mathematics, the _____ or Pythagoras' theorem is a relation in Euclidean geometry among the three sides of a right triangle. The theorem is named after the Greek mathematician Pythagoras, who by tradition is credited with its discovery and proof, although it is often argued that knowledge of the theory predates him.. The theorem is as follows:

In any right triangle, the area of the square whose side is the hypotenuse is equal to the sum of the areas of the squares whose sides are the two legs.

   a. 1-center problem
   b. Pythagorean Theorem
   c. 2-3 heap
   d. 120-cell

18. In mathematics, a _____ is a statement that can be proved on the basis of explicitly stated or previously agreed assumptions.
   a. Disjunction introduction
   b. Theorem
   c. Boolean function
   d. Logical value

Chapter 1. Problem Solving and Critical Thinking

19. A _____, from the French patron, is a type of theme of recurring events of or objects, sometimes referred to as elements of a set. These elements repeat in a predictable manner. It can be a template or model which can be used to generate things or parts of a thing, especially if the things that are created have enough in common for the underlying _____ to be inferred, in which case the things are said to exhibit the unique _____.
   - a. 1-center problem
   - b. 2-3 heap
   - c. 120-cell
   - d. Pattern

20. A _____ is a type of affix attached to a stem which modifies the meaning of that stem.

    The word '_____' is itself made up of the stem fix, and the _____ pre-, both of which are derived from Latin roots.

    - English _____es
    - _____es and suffixes in Hebrew

    - a. 120-cell
    - b. Prefix
    - c. 2-3 heap
    - d. 1-center problem

21. _____ is the mathematical operation of scaling one number by another. It is one of the four basic operations in elementary arithmetic.

    _____ is defined for whole numbers in terms of repeated addition; for example, 4 multiplied by 3 can be calculated by adding 3 copies of 4 together:

    $$4 + 4 + 4 = 12.$$

    _____ of rational numbers and real numbers is defined by systematic generalization of this basic idea.

    - a. Least common multiple
    - b. Multiplication
    - c. The number 0 is even.
    - d. Highest common factor

22. In mathematics, a _____ is the end result of a division problem. It can also be expressed as the number of times the divisor divides into the dividend.
    - a. Marginal cost
    - b. Quotient
    - c. Notation
    - d. Limiting

23. A _____ is a number that can be represented as a regular and discrete geometric pattern. If the pattern is polytopic, the figurate is labeled a polytopic number, and may be a polygonal number or a polyhedral number.

    The first few triangular numbers can be built from rows of 1, 2, 3, 4, 5, and 6 items:

    The n-th regular r-topic number is given by the formula:

    $$P_r(n) = \binom{n+r-1}{r} = \frac{n^{(r)}}{r!} \quad \text{for } n \geq 1$$

r! is the factorial of r, $\binom{n}{r}$ is a binomial coefficient, and n is the rising factorial.

a. Heptagonal number
b. Figurate number
c. Centered pentagonal number
d. Square number

24. In mathematics, a _____, sometimes also called a perfect square, is an integer that can be written as the square of some other integer; in other words, it is the product of some integer with itself. So, for example, 9 is a _____, since it can be written as 3 × 3. _____s are non-negative.

a. Centered pentagonal number
b. Hexagonal number
c. Pentagonal pyramidal number
d. Square number

25. A _____ is the sum of the n natural numbers from 1 to n.

$$T_n = 1 + 2 + 3 + \cdots + (n-1) + n = \frac{n(n+1)}{2} = \frac{n^2+n}{2} \stackrel{\text{def}}{=} \binom{n+1}{2}$$

As shown in the rightmost term of this formula, every _____ is a binomial coefficient: the nth triangular is the number of distinct pairs to be selected from n + 1 objects. In this form it solves the 'handshake problem' of counting the number of handshakes if each person in a room full of n+1 total people shakes hands once with each other person.

a. Star number
b. Centered pentagonal number
c. Triangular number
d. Heptagonal number

26. _____ is the calculated approximation of a result which is usable even if input data may be incomplete or uncertain.

In statistics, see _____ theory, estimator.

In mathematics, approximation or _____ typically means finding upper or lower bounds of a quantity that cannot readily be computed precisely and is also an educated guess .

a. Estimator
b. Estimation
c. Estimation theory
d. U-statistic

27. _____ is a numeral system in which each position is related to the next by a constant multiplier, a common ratio, called the base or radix of that numeral system.

a. Cyrillic numerals
b. NegaFibonacci coding
c. Negative base
d. Place value

28. _____ involves reducing the number of significant digits in a number. The result of _____ is a 'shorter' number having fewer non-zero digits yet similar in magnitude. The result is less precise but easier to use.

a. Sudan function
b. Rounding
c. Shabakh
d. Hyper operator

29. A _____ is a simple shape of Euclidean geometry consisting of those points in a plane which are at a constant distance, called the radius, from a fixed point, called the center. A _____ with center A is sometimes denoted by the symbol A.

A chord of a _____ is a line segment whose two endpoints lie on the _____.

a. Malfatti circles
b. Circumcircle
c. Circular segment
d. Circle

30. In graph theory, a _____ is a graph whose vertices can be associated with chords of a circle such that two vertices are adjacent if and only if the corresponding chords in the circle intersect.

Spinrad (1994) gives an $O(n^2)$-time recognition algorithm for _____s that also computes a circle model of the input graph if it is a _____.

A number of other problems that are NP-complete on general graphs have polynomial time algorithms when restricted to _____s.

a. Sparse graph
b. Circle graph
c. Planar graph
d. Vertex-transitive graph

31. A _____ is a circular chart divided into sectors, illustrating relative magnitudes or frequences or percents. In a _____, the arc length of each sector, is proportional to the quantity it represents. Together, the sectors create a full disk.
a. Pie chart
b. 2-3 heap
c. 1-center problem
d. 120-cell

32. In mathematics the concept of a _____ generalizes notions such as 'length', 'area', and 'volume'. Informally, given some base set, a '_____' is any consistent assignment of 'sizes' to the subsets of the base set. Depending on the application, the 'size' of a subset may be interpreted as its physical size, the amount of something that lies within the subset, or the probability that some random process will yield a result within the subset.
a. Measure
b. Congruent
c. Lattice
d. Cusp

33. A bar chart or _____ is a chart with rectangular bars with lengths proportional to the values that they represent. Bar charts are used for comparing two or more values. The bars can be horizontally or vertically oriented.
a. 120-cell
b. 1-center problem
c. 2-3 heap
d. Bar graph

34. In a graph theory, the _____ L

One of the earliest and most important theorems about _____s is due to Hassler Whitney, who proved that with one exceptional case the structure of G can be recovered completely from its _____.

a. Line graph
b. Vertex-transitive graph
c. Sparse graph
d. Bivariegated graph

35. In graph theory, a _____ in a graph is a sequence of vertices such that from each of its vertices there is an edge to the next vertex in the sequence. The first vertex is called the start vertex and the last vertex is called the end vertex. Both of them are called end or terminal vertices of the _____.
   a. Class
   b. Path
   c. Blinding
   d. Deltoid

36. In mathematics and in the sciences, a _____ (plural: _____e, formulæ or _____s) is a concise way of expressing information symbolically (as in a mathematical or chemical _____), or a general relationship between quantities. One of many famous _____e is Albert Einstein's E = mc² (see special relativity

In mathematics, a _____ is a key to solve an equation with variables. For example, the problem of determining the volume of a sphere is one that requires a significant amount of integral calculus to solve.

   a. Formula
   b. 1-center problem
   c. 120-cell
   d. 2-3 heap

37. A _____ is an abstract model that uses mathematical language to describe the behavior of a system. Eykhoff defined a _____ as 'a representation of the essential aspects of an existing system which presents knowledge of that system in usable form'.
   a. Rata Die
   b. Metaheuristic
   c. Mathematical model
   d. Total least squares

38. In ecology, predation describes a biological interaction where a _____ (an organism that is hunting) feeds on its prey, the organism that is attacked. _____s may or may not kill their prey prior to feeding on them, but the act of predation always results in the death of the prey. The other main category of consumption is detritivory, the consumption of dead organic material (detritus.)
   a. 120-cell
   b. 1-center problem
   c. Prey
   d. Predator

39. In mathematics, the concept of a _____ tries to capture the intuitive idea of a geometrical one-dimensional and continuous object. A simple example is the circle. In everyday use of the term '_____', a straight line is not curved, but in mathematical parlance _____s include straight lines and line segments.
   a. Negative pedal curve
   b. Quadrifolium
   c. Kappa curve
   d. Curve

40. A _____ is a 2D geometric symbolic representation of information according to some visualization technique. Sometimes, the technique uses a 3D visualization which is then projected onto the 2D surface. The word graph is sometimes used as a synonym for _____.
   a. 120-cell
   b. Diagram
   c. 2-3 heap
   d. 1-center problem

Chapter 1. Problem Solving and Critical Thinking

41. _____ or set diagrams are diagrams that show all hypothetically possible logical relations between a finite collection of sets. _____ were invented around 1880 by John Venn. They are used in many fields, including set theory, probability, logic, statistics, and computer science.
   a. 1-center problem
   b. Venn diagrams
   c. 120-cell
   d. 2-3 heap

42. In mathematics, _____ is a property that a binary operation can have. It means that, within an expression containing two or more of the same associative operators in a row, the order that the operations are performed does not matter as long as the sequence of the operands is not changed. That is, rearranging the parentheses in such an expression will not change its value.
   a. Associativity
   b. Idempotence
   c. Algebraically closed
   d. Unital

43. An _____ of order n is an arrangement of the numbers 1 to n^2 in a square, such that the n rows, the n columns and the two diagonals form a sequence of 2n + 2 consecutive integers. The smallest _____s have order 4.

In each of these two _____s of order 4, the rows, columns and diagonals sum to ten different numbers in the range 29-38.

   a. A chemical equation
   b. A posteriori
   c. A Mathematical Theory of Communication
   d. Antimagic square

44. _____ is a logic-based number-placement puzzle. The objective is to fill a 9×9 grid so that each column, each row, and each of the nine 3×3 boxes contains the digits from 1 to 9 only one time each. The puzzle setter provides a partially completed grid.
   a. Sudoku
   b. 2-3 heap
   c. 1-center problem
   d. 120-cell

45. In World War II, _____ was the United States codename for intelligence derived from the cryptanalysis of PURPLE, a Japanese foreign office cipher.

The Japanese and the Germans both used the Enigma machine to encode their cable traffic. The Japanese Enigma-based system was called PURPLE by U.S. cryptographers.

   a. Discontinuity
   b. Bandwidth
   c. Basis
   d. Magic

46. In mathematics, an _____ is a statement about the relative size or order of two objects, or about whether they are the same or not

   - The notation a < b means that a is less than b.
   - The notation a > b means that a is greater than b.
   - The notation a ≠ b means that a is not equal to b, but does not say that one is bigger than the other or even that they can be compared in size.

In all these cases, a is not equal to b, hence, '_____'.

These relations are known as strict _____

- The notation a ≤ b means that a is less than or equal to b;
- The notation a ≥ b means that a is greater than or equal to b;

An additional use of the notation is to show that one quantity is much greater than another, normally by several orders of magnitude.

- The notation a << b means that a is much less than b.
- The notation a >> b means that a is much greater than b.

If the sense of the _____ is the same for all values of the variables for which its members are defined, then the _____ is called an 'absolute' or 'unconditional' _____. If the sense of an _____ holds only for certain values of the variables involved, but is reversed or destroyed for other values of the variables, it is called a conditional _____.

An _____ may appear unsolvable because it only states whether a number is larger or smaller than another number; but it is possible to apply the same operations for equalities to inequalities. For example, to find x for the _____ 10x > 23 one would divide 23 by 10.

a. A posteriori
b. A chemical equation
c. A Mathematical Theory of Communication
d. Inequality

Chapter 2. Set Theory

1. In mathematics, an _____ or member of a set is any one of the distinct objects that make up that set.

Writing A = {1,2,3,4}, means that the _____s of the set A are the numbers 1, 2, 3 and 4. Groups of _____s of A, for example {1,2}, are subsets of A.

   a. Ideal
   b. Element
   c. Order
   d. Universal code

2. _____ or set diagrams are diagrams that show all hypothetically possible logical relations between a finite collection of sets. _____ were invented around 1880 by John Venn. They are used in many fields, including set theory, probability, logic, statistics, and computer science.

   a. 120-cell
   b. 2-3 heap
   c. 1-center problem
   d. Venn diagrams

3. In mathematics, _____ is a property that a binary operation can have. It means that, within an expression containing two or more of the same associative operators in a row, the order that the operations are performed does not matter as long as the sequence of the operands is not changed. That is, rearranging the parentheses in such an expression will not change its value.

   a. Unital
   b. Associativity
   c. Algebraically closed
   d. Idempotence

4. In mathematics, _____ and undefined are used to explain whether or not expressions have meaningful, sensible, and unambiguous values. Not all branches of mathematics come to the same conclusion.

The following expressions are undefined in all contexts, but remarks in the analysis section may apply.

   a. Defined
   b. LHS
   c. Toy model
   d. Plugging in

5. A _____ is a 2D geometric symbolic representation of information according to some visualization technique. Sometimes, the technique uses a 3D visualization which is then projected onto the 2D surface. The word graph is sometimes used as a synonym for _____.

   a. 1-center problem
   b. 2-3 heap
   c. 120-cell
   d. Diagram

6. In mathematics, and more specifically set theory, the _____ is the unique set having no members. Some axiomatic set theories assure that the _____ exists by including an axiom of _____; in other theories, its existence can be deduced. Many possible properties of sets are trivially true for the _____.

   a. A Mathematical Theory of Communication
   b. Empty function
   c. Inverse function
   d. Empty set

7. In mathematics, a _____ is a set that is negligible in some sense. For different applications, the meaning of 'negligible' varies. In measure theory, any set of measure 0 is called a _____.

   a. Null set
   b. Borel-Cantelli lemma
   c. Prevalence and shyness
   d. Radonifying function

8. In mathematics, a _____ can mean either an element of the set {1, 2, 3, ...} or an element of the set {0, 1, 2, 3, ...}. The latter is especially preferred in mathematical logic, set theory, and computer science.

_____s have two main purposes: they can be used for counting, and they can be used for ordering.

a. Suslin cardinal
b. Strong partition cardinal
c. Cardinal numbers
d. Natural number

9. In mathematics, an _____ is a statement about the relative size or order of two objects, or about whether they are the same or not

- The notation a < b means that a is less than b.
- The notation a > b means that a is greater than b.
- The notation a ≠ b means that a is not equal to b, but does not say that one is bigger than the other or even that they can be compared in size.

In all these cases, a is not equal to b, hence, '_____'.

These relations are known as strict _____

- The notation a ≤ b means that a is less than or equal to b;
- The notation a ≥ b means that a is greater than or equal to b;

An additional use of the notation is to show that one quantity is much greater than another, normally by several orders of magnitude.

- The notation a << b means that a is much less than b.
- The notation a >> b means that a is much greater than b.

If the sense of the _____ is the same for all values of the variables for which its members are defined, then the _____ is called an 'absolute' or 'unconditional' _____. If the sense of an _____ holds only for certain values of the variables involved, but is reversed or destroyed for other values of the variables, it is called a conditional _____.

An _____ may appear unsolvable because it only states whether a number is larger or smaller than another number; but it is possible to apply the same operations for equalities to inequalities. For example, to find x for the _____ 10x > 23 one would divide 23 by 10.

a. Inequality
b. A Mathematical Theory of Communication
c. A posteriori
d. A chemical equation

10. The _____ is a decimalised system of measurement. It exists in several variations, with different choices of base units, though the choice of base units does not affect its day-to-day use. Over the last two centuries, different variants have been considered the _____.

Chapter 2. Set Theory

a. George Dantzig
b. 1-center problem
c. Nonlinear system
d. Metric system

11. In mathematics, the _____ or Pythagoras' theorem is a relation in Euclidean geometry among the three sides of a right triangle. The theorem is named after the Greek mathematician Pythagoras, who by tradition is credited with its discovery and proof, although it is often argued that knowledge of the theory predates him.. The theorem is as follows:

In any right triangle, the area of the square whose side is the hypotenuse is equal to the sum of the areas of the squares whose sides are the two legs.

a. 1-center problem
b. 2-3 heap
c. 120-cell
d. Pythagorean Theorem

12. In mathematics, a _____ is a statement that can be proved on the basis of explicitly stated or previously agreed assumptions.
a. Logical value
b. Theorem
c. Boolean function
d. Disjunction introduction

13. _____ is a quantity expressing the two-dimensional size of a defined part of a surface, typically a region bounded by a closed curve. The term surface _____ refers to the total _____ of the exposed surface of a 3-dimensional solid, such as the sum of the _____s of the exposed sides of a polyhedron. _____ is an important invariant in the differential geometry of surfaces.
a. A Mathematical Theory of Communication
b. A posteriori
c. A chemical equation
d. Area

14. A _____ is a type of affix attached to a stem which modifies the meaning of that stem.

The word '_____' is itself made up of the stem fix, and the _____ pre-, both of which are derived from Latin roots.

- English _____es
- _____es and suffixes in Hebrew

a. 120-cell
b. 2-3 heap
c. Prefix
d. 1-center problem

15. In mathematics, the _____ of a set is a measure of the 'number of elements of the set'. For example, the set A = {1, 2, 3} contains 3 elements, and therefore A has a _____ of 3. There are two approaches to _____ - one which compares sets directly using bijections and injections, and another which uses cardinal numbers.
a. 120-cell
b. 2-3 heap
c. Cardinality
d. 1-center problem

16. In the study of metric spaces in mathematics, there are various notions of two metrics on the same underlying space being 'the same', or _____.

Chapter 2. Set Theory

In the following, M will denote a non-empty set and d_1 and d_2 will denote two metrics on M.

The two metrics d_1 and d_2 are said to be topologically _____ if they generate the same topology on M.

- a. A posteriori
- b. A Mathematical Theory of Communication
- c. A chemical equation
- d. Equivalent

17. In mathematics, especially in set theory, a set A is a _____ of a set B if A is 'contained' inside B. Notice that A and B may coincide. The relationship of one set being a _____ of another is called inclusion.
- a. Subset
- b. Horizontal line test
- c. Cartesian product
- d. Set of all sets

18. Exponentiation is a mathematical operation, written a^n, involving two numbers, the base a and the _____ n. When n is a positive integer, exponentiation corresponds to repeated multiplication:

$$a^n = \underbrace{a \times \cdots \times a}_{n},$$

just as multiplication by a positive integer corresponds to repeated addition:

$$a \times n = \underbrace{a + \cdots + a}_{n}.$$

The _____ is usually shown as a superscript to the right of the base. The exponentiation a^n can be read as: a raised to the n-th power, a raised to the power [of] n or possibly a raised to the _____ [of] n, or more briefly: a to the n-th power or a to the power [of] n, or even more briefly: a to the n.

- a. Exponentiating by squaring
- b. Exponential tree
- c. Exponential sum
- d. Exponent

19. In mathematics, _____ are generalized numbers used to measure the cardinality of sets. For finite sets, the cardinality is given by a natural number, which is simply the number of elements in the set. There are also transfinite _____ that describe the sizes of infinite sets.
- a. Cardinality of the continuum
- b. Suslin cardinal
- c. Strong partition cardinal
- d. Cardinal numbers

20. In computational complexity theory, an algorithm is said to take _____ if the asymptotic upper bound for the time it requires is proportional to the size of the input, which is usually denoted n.

Informally spoken, the running time increases linearly with the size of the input. For example, a procedure that adds up all elements of a list requires time proportional to the length of the list.

a. Time-constructible function
b. Linear time
c. Truth table reduction
d. Constructible function

21. In mathematics, two sets are said to be disjoint if they have no element in common. For example, {1, 2, 3} and {4, 5, 6} are _____.

Formally, two sets A and B are disjoint if their intersection is the empty set.
wikimedia.org/math/b/3/5/b35d3befc06b831ff4d6cd63bf922efb.png">

This definition extends to any collection of sets.

a. Subset
b. Horizontal line test
c. Preimage
d. Disjoint sets

22. In discrete mathematics and predominantly in set theory, a _____ is a concept used in comparisons of sets to refer to the unique values of one set in relation to another. The terms 'absolute' and 'relative' _____ refer to more specific applications of the concept, with universal _____s referring to elements unique to the universal set and the latter referring to the unique elements of one set in relation to another. In this image, the universal set is represented by the border of the image, and the set A as a disc.

a. Complement
b. Derivative algebra
c. Huge
d. Kernel

23. In mathematics, the _____ of two sets A and B is the set that contains all elements of A that also belong to B, but no other elements.

For explanation of the symbols used in this article, refer to the table of mathematical symbols.

The _____ of A and B

The _____ of A and B is written 'A ∩ B'. Formally:

> x is an element of A ∩ B if and only if
> - x is an element of A and
> - x is an element of B.
>
> For example:
> - The _____ of the sets {1, 2, 3} and {2, 3, 4} is {2, 3}.
> - The number 9 is not in the _____ of the set of prime numbers {2, 3, 5, 7, 11, …} and the set of odd numbers {1, 3, 5, 7, 9, 11, …}.

If the _____ of two sets A and B is empty, that is they have no elements in common, then they are said to be disjoint, denoted: A ∩ B = ∅. For example the sets {1, 2} and {3, 4} are disjoint, written {1, 2} ∩ {3, 4} = ∅.

a. Intersection
c. Advice
b. Order
d. Erlang

24. In set theory, the term _____ refers to a set operation used in the convergence of set elements to form a resultant set containing the elements of both sets. As a simple example, a _____ of two disjoint sets, which do not have elements in common results in a set containing all elements from both sets. A Venn diagram representing the _____ of sets A and B.
   a. UES
   b. Introduction
   c. Event
   d. Union

25. In graph theory, a _____ is a digraph with weighted edges. These _____s have become an especially useful concept in analysing the interaction between biology and mathematics. Using _____s of all types; various applications based on the creativity of the mathematician along with their environment can be evaluated in all sorts of manners.
   a. Network
   b. Copula
   c. Colossus
   d. Chord

26. _____ consists of mental processes of discernment, analysis and evaluation. It includes possible processes of reflecting upon a tangible or intangible item in order to form a solid judgment that reconciles scientific evidence with common sense. In contemporary usage 'critical' has a certain negative connotation that does not apply in the present case.
   a. Counterpart theory
   b. Finite model property
   c. Parametric operator
   d. Critical thinking

27. Induction or _____, sometimes called inductive logic, is the process of reasoning in which the premises of an argument are believed to support the conclusion but do not entail it;. Induction is a form of reasoning that makes generalizations based on individual instances. It is used to ascribe properties or relations to types based on an observation instance; or to formulate laws based on limited observations of recurring phenomenal patterns.
   a. Affine logic
   b. Inductive reasoning
   c. Idempotency of entailment
   d. Intuitionistic logic

Chapter 3. Logic

1. _____ is the study of the principles of valid demonstration and inference. _____ is a branch of philosophy, a part of the classical trivium of grammar, _____, and rhetoric. of λογικῌΟες, 'possessed of reason, intellectual, dialectical, argumentative', from λῙΟεγος logos, 'word, thought, idea, argument, account, reason, or principle'.
   - a. Logic
   - b. Satisfiability
   - c. Boolean function
   - d. Counterpart theory

2. In logic and mathematics, _____ or not is an operation on logical values, for example, the logical value of a proposition, that sends true to false and false to true. Intuitively, the _____ of a proposition holds exactly when that proposition does not hold. In grammar, nor is an adverb which acts as a coordinating conjunction.
   - a. 1-center problem
   - b. Negation
   - c. Syntax
   - d. Sentence diagram

3. In mathematics, _____ and undefined are used to explain whether or not expressions have meaningful, sensible, and unambiguous values. Not all branches of mathematics come to the same conclusion.

   The following expressions are undefined in all contexts, but remarks in the analysis section may apply.
   - a. Toy model
   - b. Defined
   - c. LHS
   - d. Plugging in

4. _____, in logic and fields that rely on it such as mathematics and philosophy, is a biconditional logical connective between statements. In that it is biconditional, the connective can be likened to the standard material conditional ('if') combined with its reverse ('only if'); hence the name. The result is that the truth of either one of the connected statements requires the truth of the other.
   - a. Enumerative definition
   - b. Existential graph
   - c. Algebraic logic
   - d. If and only if

5. In abstract algebra, a module S over a ring R is called _____ or irreducible if it is not the zero module 0 and if its only submodules are 0 and S. Understanding the _____ modules over a ring is usually helpful because these modules form the 'building blocks' of all other modules in a certain sense.

   Abelian groups are the same as Z-modules.
   - a. Simple
   - b. Derivation
   - c. Basis
   - d. Harmonic series

6. In logic and mathematics, or, also known as logical _____ or inclusive _____ is a logical operator that results in true whenever one or more of its operands are true. In grammar, or is a coordinating conjunction. In ordinary language 'or' rather has the meaning of exclusive _____.
   - a. Triquetra
   - b. Cube
   - c. Zero-point energy
   - d. Disjunction

7. An _____ is one that cannot be compressed because it lacks sufficient repeating sequences. Whether a string is compressible will often depend on the algorithm being used. Some examples may illuminate this.
   - a. Arithmetic coding
   - b. A Mathematical Theory of Communication
   - c. Entropy encoding
   - d. Incompressible string

Chapter 3. Logic

8. In propositional logic, a set of Boolean operators is called _____ if it permits the realisation of any possible truth table.

Using a complete Boolean algebra which does not include XOR (such as the well-known AND OR NOT set), this function can be realised as follows:

(a or b) and not (a and b.)

However, other complete Boolean algebras are possible, such as NAND or NOR (either gate can form a complete Boolean algebra by itself - the proof is detailed on their pages.)

a. Sufficient
b. Counterfactual conditional
c. First-order predicate calculus
d. Logical biconditional

9. In game theory, _____ occurs when one strategy is better than another strategy for one player, no matter how that player's opponents may play. Many simple games can be solved using _____. The opposite, intransitivity, occurs in games where one strategy may be better or worse than another strategy for one player, depending on how the player's opponents may play.

a. Dominance
b. Coherence
c. Boolean algebra
d. Concurrent

10. A _____ is a mathematical table used in logic -- specifically in connection with Boolean algebra, boolean functions, and propositional calculus -- to compute the functional values of logical expressions on each of their functional arguments, that is, on each combination of values taken by their logical variables. In particular, _____s can be used to tell whether a propositional expression is true for all legitimate input values, that is, logically valid.

The pattern of reasoning that the _____ tabulates was Frege's, Peirce's, and Schröder's by 1880.

a. Truth table
b. 120-cell
c. 2-3 heap
d. 1-center problem

11. In computational complexity theory, an algorithm is said to take _____ if the asymptotic upper bound for the time it requires is proportional to the size of the input, which is usually denoted n.

Informally spoken, the running time increases linearly with the size of the input. For example, a procedure that adds up all elements of a list requires time proportional to the length of the list.

a. Time-constructible function
b. Truth table reduction
c. Linear time
d. Constructible function

12. The _____ fallacy is an informal fallacy. It ascribes cause where none exists. The flaw is failing to account for natural fluctuations.

a. Differential
b. Degrees of freedom
c. Depth
d. Regression

13. In the study of metric spaces in mathematics, there are various notions of two metrics on the same underlying space being 'the same', or _____.

In the following, M will denote a non-empty set and d_1 and d_2 will denote two metrics on M.

The two metrics d_1 and d_2 are said to be topologically _____ if they generate the same topology on M.

a. A posteriori
b. A chemical equation
c. Equivalent
d. A Mathematical Theory of Communication

14. In propositional logic, contraposition is a logical relationship between two statements of material implication. A proposition Q is materially implied by a proposition P when the following relationship holds:

$$(P \rightarrow Q)$$

In vernacular terms, this states 'If P then Q', or, 'If Socrates is a man then Socrates is human.' In a conditional such as this, P is called the antecedent and Q the consequent. One statement is the _____ of the other just when its antecedent is the negated consequent of the other, and vice-versa.

a. Control chart
b. Continuous signal
c. Contour map
d. Contrapositive

15. In mathematics, the _____ of a number n is the number that, when added to n, yields zero. The _____ of n is denoted −n. For example, 7 is −7, because 7 + (−7) = 0, and the _____ of −0.3 is 0.3, because −0.3 + 0.3 = 0.

a. Algebraic structure
b. Associativity
c. Additive inverse
d. Arity

16. In mathematics, a _____ is a statement that can be proved on the basis of explicitly stated or previously agreed assumptions.

a. Boolean function
b. Logical value
c. Disjunction introduction
d. Theorem

17. In mathematics, and particularly in applications to set theory and the foundations of mathematics, a _____ or universal class is a class that contains all of the elements and sets that one may wish to use in a given situation. There are several versions of this general idea, described in the following sections.

Perhaps the simplest version is that any set can be a _____, so long as the object of study is confined to that particular set.

a. A chemical equation
b. Universe
c. A Mathematical Theory of Communication
d. Operation

18. In vector calculus, _____ is a vector differential operator represented by the nabla symbol: ∇.

_____ is a mathematical tool serving primarily as a convention for mathematical notation; it makes many equations easier to comprehend, write, and remember. Depending on the way _____ is applied, it can describe the gradient (slope), divergence (degree to which something converges or diverges) or curl (rotational motion at points in a fluid.)

a. Del
b. Vector field reconstruction
c. Helmholtz decomposition
d. Del operator

19. A _____ is a 2D geometric symbolic representation of information according to some visualization technique. Sometimes, the technique uses a 3D visualization which is then projected onto the 2D surface. The word graph is sometimes used as a synonym for _____.
a. Diagram
b. 2-3 heap
c. 1-center problem
d. 120-cell

20. _____ consists of mental processes of discernment, analysis and evaluation. It includes possible processes of reflecting upon a tangible or intangible item in order to form a solid judgment that reconciles scientific evidence with common sense. In contemporary usage 'critical' has a certain negative connotation that does not apply in the present case.
a. Parametric operator
b. Finite model property
c. Counterpart theory
d. Critical thinking

21. In psychology, _____ has two distinct fields of application. The first involves test _____, a concept that has evolved with the field of psychometrics but which textbooks still commonly gloss over in explaining that it is the degree to which a test measures what it was designed to measure. The second involves research design.
a. Finitism
b. Validity
c. Model theory
d. Modal logic

22. _____, also sometimes known as standard form or as exponential notation, is a way of writing numbers that accommodates values too large or small to be conveniently written in standard decimal notation. _____ has a number of useful properties and is often favored by scientists, mathematicians and engineers, who work with such numbers.

In _____, numbers are written in the form:

$$a \times 10^b$$

a. Radix point
b. Leading zero
c. 1-center problem
d. Scientific notation

23. _____ is used to describe the steepness, incline, gradient, or grade of a straight line. A higher _____ value indicates a steeper incline. The _____ is defined as the ratio of the 'rise' divided by the 'run' between two points on a line, or in other words, the ratio of the altitude change to the horizontal distance between any two points on the line.
a. Cognitively Guided Instruction
b. Slope
c. Number line
d. Point plotting

24. In vascular plants, the _____ is the organ of a plant body that typically lies below the surface of the soil. This is not always the case, however, since a _____ can also be aerial (that is, growing above the ground) or aerating (that is, growing up above the ground or especially above water.) Furthermore, a stem normally occurring below ground is not exceptional either

   a. 1-center problem   b. Root
   c. 2-3 heap   d. 120-cell

Chapter 4. Number Representation and Calculation

1. Exponentiation is a mathematical operation, written a^n, involving two numbers, the base a and the _____ n. When n is a positive integer, exponentiation corresponds to repeated multiplication:

$$a^n = \underbrace{a \times \cdots \times a}_{n},$$

just as multiplication by a positive integer corresponds to repeated addition:

$$a \times n = \underbrace{a + \cdots + a}_{n}.$$

The _____ is usually shown as a superscript to the right of the base. The exponentiation a^n can be read as: a raised to the n-th power, a raised to the power [of] n or possibly a raised to the _____ [of] n, or more briefly: a to the n-th power or a to the power [of] n, or even more briefly: a to the n.

   a. Exponent   b. Exponential sum
   c. Exponentiating by squaring   d. Exponential tree

2. Scientific notation, also sometimes known as standard form or as _____, is a way of writing numbers that accommodates values too large or small to be conveniently written in standard decimal notation. Scientific notation has a number of useful properties and is often favored by scientists, mathematicians and engineers, who work with such numbers.

In scientific notation, numbers are written in the form:

$$a \times 10^b$$

   a. A chemical equation   b. A posteriori
   c. A Mathematical Theory of Communication   d. Exponential notation

3. In mathematics, _____ and undefined are used to explain whether or not expressions have meaningful, sensible, and unambiguous values. Not all branches of mathematics come to the same conclusion.

The following expressions are undefined in all contexts, but remarks in the analysis section may apply.

   a. Defined   b. Toy model
   c. LHS   d. Plugging in

4. _____ is simply the manner of writing out an expression in full. When a quantity is written as a sum of terms, or as a continued product, _____ notation is used to illustrate the expression in its entirety.

   a. Algebra   b. Algebraic function
   c. Expanded form   d. Algebraic element

5. In mathematics, the _____ is a term used to describe the number of times one must apply a given operation to an integer before reaching a fixed point.

Usually, this refers to the additive or multiplicative persistence of an integer, which is how often one has to replace the number by the sum or product of its digits until one reaches a single digit. Because the numbers are broken down into their digits, the additive or multiplicative persistence depends on the radix.

   a. Lychrel number
   b. Coprime
   c. Linear congruence theorem
   d. Persistence of a number

6. Leonardo of Pisa (c. 1170 - c. 1250), also known as Leonardo Pisano, Leonardo Bonacci, Leonardo _____, or, most commonly, simply _____, was an Italian mathematician, considered by some 'the most talented mathematician of the Middle Ages'.
   a. Guido Castelnuovo
   b. Fibonacci
   c. Harry Hinsley
   d. Ralph C. Merkle

7. In cryptography, _____ is a pseudorandom number generator and a stream cipher designed by Robert Jenkins to be cryptographically secure. The name is an acronym for Indirection, Shift, Accumulate, Add, and Count.

The _____ algorithm has similarities with RC4.

   a. Order
   b. Introduction
   c. Imputation
   d. Isaac

8. In mathematics, a _____ is a number which can be expressed as a ratio of two integers. Non-integer _____s are usually written as the vulgar fraction $\frac{a}{b}$, where b is not zero. a is called the numerator, and b the denominator.
   a. Rational number
   b. Minkowski distance
   c. Tally marks
   d. Pre-algebra

9. In mathematics and computer science, _____ (also base-16, hexa or base, of 16. It uses sixteen distinct symbols, most often the symbols 0-9 to represent values zero to nine, and A, B, C, D, E, F (or a through f) to represent values ten to fifteen.

Its primary use is as a human friendly representation of binary coded values, so it is often used in digital electronics and computer engineering.

   a. Tetradecimal
   b. Factoradic
   c. Radix
   d. Hexadecimal

10. A _____ system uses discrete (discontinuous) values, usually but not always symbolized numerically (hence called '_____') to represent information for input, processing, transmission, storage, etc. By contrast, non-_____ (or analog) systems use a continuous range of values to represent information. Although _____ representations are discrete, the information represented can be either discrete, such as numbers, letters or icons, or continuous, such as sounds, images, and other measurements of continuous systems.
   a. 2-3 heap
   b. 120-cell
   c. 1-center problem
   d. Digital

Chapter 4. Number Representation and Calculation

11. A _____ typically refers to a class of handheld calculators that are capable of plotting graphs, solving simultaneous equations, and performing numerous other tasks with variables. Most popular _____s are also programmable, allowing the user to create customized programs, typically for scientific/engineering and education applications. Due to their large displays intended for graphing, they can also accommodate several lines of text and calculations at a time.
   a. Graphing calculator
   b. Support vector machines
   c. Bump mapping
   d. Genus

12. A _____ is a device for performing mathematical calculations, distinguished from a computer by having a limited problem solving ability and an interface optimized for interactive calculation rather than programming. _____s can be hardware or software, and mechanical or electronic, and are often built into devices such as PDAs or mobile phones.

   Modern electronic _____s are generally small, digital, and usually inexpensive.

   a. 120-cell
   b. 1-center problem
   c. 2-3 heap
   d. Calculator

13. The _____ are the set of numbers consisting of the natural numbers including 0 and their negatives. They are numbers that can be written without a fractional or decimal component, and fall within the set {... −2, −1, 0, 1, 2, ...}.
   a. Integers
   b. A posteriori
   c. A Mathematical Theory of Communication
   d. A chemical equation

14. The _____ numeral system is the base-8 number system, and uses the digits 0 to 7. Numerals can be made from binary numerals by grouping consecutive digits into groups of three (starting from the right.) For example, the binary representation for decimal 74 is 1001010, which groups into 001 001 010 -- so the _____ representation is 112.
   a. A posteriori
   b. A chemical equation
   c. A Mathematical Theory of Communication
   d. Octal

15. In the mathematical area of order theory, the _____ or finite elements of a partially ordered set are those elements that cannot be subsumed by a supremum of any non-empty directed set that does not already contain members above the _____ element.

Note that there are other notions of compactness in mathematics; also, the term 'finite' in its normal set theoretic meaning does not coincide with the order-theoretic notion of a 'finite element'.

In a partially ordered set an element c is called _____ if it satisfies one of the following equivalent conditions:

- For every nonempty directed subset D of P, if D has a supremum sup D and c ≤ sup D then c ≤ d for some element d of D.
- For every ideal I of P, if I has a supremum sup I and c ≤ sup I then c is an element of I.

If the poset P additionally is a join-semilattice then these conditions are equivalent to the following statement:

- For every nonempty subset S of P, if S has a supremum sup S and c ≤ sup S, then c ≤ sup T for some finite subset T of S.

24 *Chapter 4. Number Representation and Calculation*

In particular, if c = sup S, then c is the supremum of a finite subset of S.

a. Train track
b. Matching distance
c. Locally regular space
d. Compact

16. _____ is an art form whose medium is sound organized in time. Common elements of _____ are pitch (which governs melody and harmony), rhythm (and its associated concepts tempo, meter, and articulation), dynamics, and the sonic qualities of timbre and texture.

The creation, performance, significance, and even the definition of _____ vary according to culture and social context.

a. 120-cell
b. 2-3 heap
c. 1-center problem
d. Music

17. In mathematics, _____ is a property that a binary operation can have. It means that, within an expression containing two or more of the same associative operators in a row, the order that the operations are performed does not matter as long as the sequence of the operands is not changed. That is, rearranging the parentheses in such an expression will not change its value.

a. Unital
b. Algebraically closed
c. Idempotence
d. Associativity

18. _____ is a general term for any type of information processing. This includes phenomena ranging from human thinking to calculations with a more narrow meaning. _____ is a process following a well-defined model that is understood and can be expressed in an algorithm, protocol, network topology, etc.

a. 1-center problem
b. 120-cell
c. 2-3 heap
d. Computation

19. The _____ is a barcode symbology, that is widely used in the United States and Canada for tracking trade items in stores. In the _____-A barcode, each digit is represented by a seven-bit sequence, encoded by a series of alternating bars and spaces. Guard bars, shown in green, separate the two groups of six digits.

The _____ encodes 12 decimal digits as SLLLLLLMRRRRRRE, where S and E are the bit pattern 101, M is the bit pattern 01010, and each L and R are digits, each one represented by a seven-bit code.

a. Universal product code
b. A posteriori
c. A Mathematical Theory of Communication
d. A chemical equation

Chapter 4. Number Representation and Calculation

20. In cryptography, the _____ was a method devised by Polish mathematician-cryptologist Jerzy Różycki, at the Polish General Staff's Cipher Bureau, to facilitate decrypting German Enigma messages. This method sometimes made it possible to determine which of the Enigma machine's rotors was at the far right, that is, in the position where the rotor always revolved at every depression of a key.

- Biuro Szyfrów

a. FROSTBURG
c. Bombe
b. TWIRL
d. Clock

21. In information theory, a _____ is a function mapping an alphabet to non-negative real numbers, satisfying a generalization of Kraft's inequality. A _____ page, a type of character encoding table, is one such _____.
   a. Code
   c. File Camouflage
   b. Deterministic encryption
   d. Link encryption

22. _____ is the mathematical operation of scaling one number by another. It is one of the four basic operations in elementary arithmetic.

_____ is defined for whole numbers in terms of repeated addition; for example, 4 multiplied by 3 can be calculated by adding 3 copies of 4 together:

$$4 + 4 + 4 = 12.$$

_____ of rational numbers and real numbers is defined by systematic generalization of this basic idea.

a. Multiplication
c. Highest common factor
b. Least common multiple
d. The number 0 is even.

23. In mathematics, a _____ is the end result of a division problem. It can also be expressed as the number of times the divisor divides into the dividend.
   a. Marginal cost
   c. Notation
   b. Limiting
   d. Quotient

24. _____ is the study of the principles of valid demonstration and inference. _____ is a branch of philosophy, a part of the classical trivium of grammar, _____, and rhetoric. of λογικ῏Œς, 'possessed of reason, intellectual, dialectical, argumentative', from λῒŒγος logos, 'word, thought, idea, argument, account, reason, or principle'.
   a. Boolean function
   c. Satisfiability
   b. Logic
   d. Counterpart theory

Chapter 5. Number Theory and the Real Number System

1. _____ is the branch of pure mathematics concerned with the properties of numbers in general, and integers in particular, as well as the wider classes of problems that arise from their study.

   _____ may be subdivided into several fields, according to the methods used and the type of questions investigated.

   The term 'arithmetic' is also used to refer to _____.

   a. Goormaghtigh conjecture
   b. Number theory
   c. Coin problem
   d. Sociable number

2. _____ is that which is owed; usually referencing assets owed, but the term can cover other obligations. In the case of assets, _____ is a means of using future purchasing power in the present before a summation has been earned.
   a. Cobb-Douglas
   b. Metaheuristic
   c. Point-slope form
   d. Debt

3. The word _____ has many distinct meanings in different fields of knowledge, depending on their methodologies and the context of discussion. Broadly speaking we can say that a _____ is some kind of belief or claim that (supposedly) explains, asserts, or consolidates some class of claims. Additionally, in contrast with a theorem the statement of the _____ is generally accepted only in some tentative fashion as opposed to regarding it as having been conclusively established.
   a. Defined
   b. Per mil
   c. Transport of structure
   d. Theory

4. _____ is the mathematical operation of scaling one number by another. It is one of the four basic operations in elementary arithmetic.

   _____ is defined for whole numbers in terms of repeated addition; for example, 4 multiplied by 3 can be calculated by adding 3 copies of 4 together:

   $$4 + 4 + 4 = 12.$$

   _____ of rational numbers and real numbers is defined by systematic generalization of this basic idea.

   a. Multiplication
   b. Highest common factor
   c. Least common multiple
   d. The number 0 is even.

5. In mathematics, a _____ can mean either an element of the set {1, 2, 3, ...} or an element of the set {0, 1, 2, 3, ...}. The latter is especially preferred in mathematical logic, set theory, and computer science.

   _____s have two main purposes: they can be used for counting, and they can be used for ordering.

   a. Cardinal numbers
   b. Natural number
   c. Strong partition cardinal
   d. Suslin cardinal

6. _____ or set diagrams are diagrams that show all hypothetically possible logical relations between a finite collection of sets. _____ were invented around 1880 by John Venn. They are used in many fields, including set theory, probability, logic, statistics, and computer science.
   a. 1-center problem
   b. 120-cell
   c. 2-3 heap
   d. Venn diagrams

7. In mathematics, _____ is a property that a binary operation can have. It means that, within an expression containing two or more of the same associative operators in a row, the order that the operations are performed does not matter as long as the sequence of the operands is not changed. That is, rearranging the parentheses in such an expression will not change its value.
   a. Unital
   b. Algebraically closed
   c. Idempotence
   d. Associativity

8. A _____ is a device for performing mathematical calculations, distinguished from a computer by having a limited problem solving ability and an interface optimized for interactive calculation rather than programming. _____s can be hardware or software, and mechanical or electronic, and are often built into devices such as PDAs or mobile phones.

   Modern electronic _____s are generally small, digital, and usually inexpensive.

   a. 2-3 heap
   b. 120-cell
   c. 1-center problem
   d. Calculator

9. In mathematics, _____ and undefined are used to explain whether or not expressions have meaningful, sensible, and unambiguous values. Not all branches of mathematics come to the same conclusion.

   The following expressions are undefined in all contexts, but remarks in the analysis section may apply.

   a. LHS
   b. Defined
   c. Toy model
   d. Plugging in

10. A _____ is a 2D geometric symbolic representation of information according to some visualization technique. Sometimes, the technique uses a 3D visualization which is then projected onto the 2D surface. The word graph is sometimes used as a synonym for _____.
    a. 2-3 heap
    b. 1-center problem
    c. Diagram
    d. 120-cell

11. In mathematics, a _____ of an integer n is an integer which evenly divides n without leaving a remainder.

    For example, 7 is a _____ of 42 because 42/7 = 6. We also say 42 is divisible by 7 or 42 is a multiple of 7 or 7 divides 42 or 7 is a factor of 42 and we usually write 7 | 42.

    a. 1-center problem
    b. 120-cell
    c. 2-3 heap
    d. Divisor

12. A _____ number is a positive integer which has a positive divisor other than one or itself. By definition, every integer greater than one is either a prime number or a _____ number. zero and one are considered to be neither prime nor _____. For example, the integer 14 is a _____ number because it can be factored as 2 × 7.
   a. Key server
   b. Composite
   c. Basis
   d. Discontinuity

13. A _____ is a positive integer which has a positive divisor other than one or itself. In other words, if 0 < n is an integer and there are integers 1 < a, b < n such that n = a × b then n is composite. By definition, every integer greater than one is either a prime number or a _____.
   a. Ruth-Aaron pair
   b. Prime Pages
   c. Megaprime
   d. Composite number

14. A _____ typically refers to a class of handheld calculators that are capable of plotting graphs, solving simultaneous equations, and performing numerous other tasks with variables. Most popular _____s are also programmable, allowing the user to create customized programs, typically for scientific/engineering and education applications. Due to their large displays intended for graphing, they can also accommodate several lines of text and calculations at a time.
   a. Bump mapping
   b. Support vector machines
   c. Genus
   d. Graphing calculator

15. In mathematics, a _____ is a natural number which has exactly two distinct natural number divisors: 1 and itself. An infinitude of _____s exists, as demonstrated by Euclid around 300 BC. The first twenty-five _____s are:

   2, 3, 5, 7, 11, 13, 17, 19, 23, 29, 31, 37, 41, 43, 47, 53, 59, 61, 67, 71, 73, 79, 83, 89, 97.

   a. Highly composite number
   b. Perrin number
   c. Pronic number
   d. Prime number

16. The _____ are the set of numbers consisting of the natural numbers including 0 and their negatives. They are numbers that can be written without a fractional or decimal component, and fall within the set {... −2, −1, 0, 1, 2, ...}.
   a. A posteriori
   b. A Mathematical Theory of Communication
   c. Integers
   d. A chemical equation

17. In number theory, the _____ states that every natural number greater than 1 can be written as a unique product of prime numbers. For instance,

$$6936 = 2^3 \times 3 \times 17^2,$$
$$1200 = 2^4 \times 3 \times 5^2.$$

There are no other possible factorizations of 6936 or 1200 into non-negative prime numbers. The above representation collapses repeated prime factors into powers for easier identification.

Chapter 5. Number Theory and the Real Number System

a. Cyclic number
b. Feit–Thompson theorem
c. Dedekind sums
d. Fundamental Theorem of Arithmetic

18. In mathematics, the _____, sometimes known as the greatest common factor or highest common factor, of two non-zero integers, is the largest positive integer that divides both numbers without remainder.

This notion can be extended to polynomials, see _____ of two polynomials.

The _____ of a and b is written as gc, or sometimes simply as.

a. Highest common factor
b. Minuend
c. Multiplication
d. Greatest common divisor

19. In mathematics, a _____ is a number which can be expressed as a ratio of two integers. Non-integer _____s are usually written as the vulgar fraction $\frac{a}{b}$, where b is not zero. a is called the numerator, and b the denominator.

a. Tally marks
b. Pre-algebra
c. Minkowski distance
d. Rational number

20. In mathematics, a _____ is a statement that can be proved on the basis of explicitly stated or previously agreed assumptions.

a. Boolean function
b. Logical value
c. Disjunction introduction
d. Theorem

21. In set theory, a _____ is a partially ordered set such that for each t ∈ T, the set {s ∈ T : s < t} is well-ordered by the relation <. For each t ∈ T, the order type of {s ∈ T : s < t} is called the height of t. The height of T itself is the least ordinal greater than the height of each element of T.

a. Definable numbers
b. Transitive reduction
c. Tree
d. Set-theoretic topology

22. In mathematics, a _____ is a mathematical statement which appears resourceful, but has not been formally proven to be true under the rules of mathematical logic. Once a _____ is formally proven true it is elevated to the status of theorem and may be used afterwards without risk in the construction of other formal mathematical proofs. Until that time, mathematicians may use the _____ on a provisional basis, but any resulting work is itself provisional until the underlying _____ is cleared up.

a. Whitehead conjecture
b. Moral certainty
c. Heawood conjecture
d. Conjecture

23. In arithmetic and number theory, the _____ or lowest common multiple or smallest common multiple of two integers a and b is the smallest positive integer that is a multiple of both a and b. Since it is a multiple, it can be divided by a and b without a remainder. If either a or b is 0, so that there is no such positive integer, then lc is defined to be zero.

a. Lowest common denominator
b. Plus-minus sign
c. Least common multiple
d. Plus and minus signs

24. In mathematics, a Mersenne number is a positive integer that is one less than a power of two:

Chapter 5. Number Theory and the Real Number System

$$M_n = 2^n - 1.$$

Some definitions of Mersenne numbers require that the exponent n be prime.

A _____ is a Mersenne number that is prime. As of October 2008, only 46 _____ s are known; the largest known prime number ($2^{43,112,609} - 1$) is a _____, and in modern times, the largest known prime has almost always been a _____.

- a. 1-center problem
- b. Mersenne number
- c. Red-black tree
- d. Mersenne prime

25. An _____ (prime spelled backwards) is a prime number that results in a different prime when its digits are reversed. This definition excludes the related palindromic primes. _____ s are also called reversible primes.
    - a. A Mathematical Theory of Communication
    - b. Octagonal number
    - c. A chemical equation
    - d. Emirp

26. In mathematics, in the realm of group theory, a group is said to be _____ if it equals its own commutator subgroup if the group has no nontrivial abelian quotients.

The smallest _____ group is the alternating group A_5. More generally, any non-abelian simple group is _____ since the commutator subgroup is a normal subgroup with abelian quotient.

- a. Group of Lie type
- b. Quaternion group
- c. Free product
- d. Perfect

27. In mathematics, a _____ is defined as a positive integer which is the sum of its proper positive divisors, that is, the sum of the positive divisors excluding the number itself. Equivalently, a _____ is a number that is half the sum of all of its positive divisors, or = 2n.

The first _____ is 6, because 1, 2, and 3 are its proper positive divisors, and 1 + 2 + 3 = 6.

- a. Blum integer
- b. Leonardo numbers
- c. Nonhypotenuse number
- d. Perfect number

28. In mathematics, _____ of order k of functions is an equivalence relation, corresponding to having the same value at a point P and also the same derivatives there, up to order k. The equivalence classes are generally called jets. The point of osculation is also called the double cusp.
    - a. Critical point
    - b. Characteristic
    - c. Dominance
    - d. Contact

29. In mathematics, a _____ is a picture of a straight line in which the integers are shown as specially-marked points evenly spaced on the line. Although this image only shows the integers from -9 to 9, the line includes all real numbers, continuing 'forever' in each direction. It is often used as an aid in teaching simple addition and subtraction, especially involving negative numbers.

Chapter 5. Number Theory and the Real Number System

a. Number line
c. Number system
b. Real number
d. Point plotting

30. In mathematics, a _____ can mean either an element of the set {1, 2, 3, ...} (i.e the positive integers) or an element of the set {0, 1, 2, 3, ...} (i.e. the non-negative integers).
    a. FISH
    b. Bounded
    c. Degrees of freedom
    d. Whole number

31. In graph theory, a _____ in a graph is a sequence of vertices such that from each of its vertices there is an edge to the next vertex in the sequence. The first vertex is called the start vertex and the last vertex is called the end vertex. Both of them are called end or terminal vertices of the _____.
    a. Deltoid
    b. Class
    c. Blinding
    d. Path

32. In mathematics, an _____ is a statement about the relative size or order of two objects, or about whether they are the same or not

    - The notation a < b means that a is less than b.
    - The notation a > b means that a is greater than b.
    - The notation a ≠ b means that a is not equal to b, but does not say that one is bigger than the other or even that they can be compared in size.

    In all these cases, a is not equal to b, hence, '_____'.

    These relations are known as strict _____

    - The notation a ≤ b means that a is less than or equal to b;
    - The notation a ≥ b means that a is greater than or equal to b;

    An additional use of the notation is to show that one quantity is much greater than another, normally by several orders of magnitude.

    - The notation a << b means that a is much less than b.
    - The notation a >> b means that a is much greater than b.

    If the sense of the _____ is the same for all values of the variables for which its members are defined, then the _____ is called an 'absolute' or 'unconditional' _____. If the sense of an _____ holds only for certain values of the variables involved, but is reversed or destroyed for other values of the variables, it is called a conditional _____.

    An _____ may appear unsolvable because it only states whether a number is larger or smaller than another number; but it is possible to apply the same operations for equalities to inequalities. For example, to find x for the _____ 10x > 23 one would divide 23 by 10.

a. Inequality
b. A posteriori
c. A Mathematical Theory of Communication
d. A chemical equation

33. In mathematics, the _____ of a real number is its numerical value without regard to its sign. So, for example, 3 is the _____ of both 3 and −3.

The _____ of a number a is denoted by $|a|$.

Generalizations of the _____ for real numbers occur in a wide variety of mathematical settings.

a. A chemical equation
b. A Mathematical Theory of Communication
c. Absolute value
d. Area hyperbolic functions

34. In mathematics, the _____ of a number n is the number that, when added to n, yields zero. The _____ of n is denoted −n. For example, 7 is −7, because 7 + (−7) = 0, and the _____ of −0.3 is 0.3, because −0.3 + 0.3 = 0.
a. Arity
b. Associativity
c. Additive inverse
d. Algebraic structure

35. In cryptography, the _____ was a method devised by Polish mathematician-cryptologist Jerzy Różycki, at the Polish General Staff's Cipher Bureau, to facilitate decrypting German Enigma messages. This method sometimes made it possible to determine which of the Enigma machine's rotors was at the far right, that is, in the position where the rotor always revolved at every depression of a key.

- Biuro Szyfrów

a. FROSTBURG
b. TWIRL
c. Bombe
d. Clock

36. In mathematics, a _____ is the end result of a division problem. It can also be expressed as the number of times the divisor divides into the dividend.
a. Notation
b. Limiting
c. Marginal cost
d. Quotient

37. Scientific notation, also sometimes known as standard form or as _____, is a way of writing numbers that accommodates values too large or small to be conveniently written in standard decimal notation. Scientific notation has a number of useful properties and is often favored by scientists, mathematicians and engineers, who work with such numbers.

In scientific notation, numbers are written in the form:

$$a \times 10^b$$

a. A Mathematical Theory of Communication
b. A chemical equation
c. Exponential notation
d. A posteriori

38. In mathematics and computer science, _____ (also base-16, hexa or base, of 16. It uses sixteen distinct symbols, most often the symbols 0-9 to represent values zero to nine, and A, B, C, D, E, F (or a through f) to represent values ten to fifteen.

Its primary use is as a human friendly representation of binary coded values, so it is often used in digital electronics and computer engineering.

a. Tetradecimal
b. Hexadecimal
c. Radix
d. Factoradic

39. In mathematics, an _____ in the sense of ring theory is a subring $\mathcal{O}$ of a ring R that satisfies the conditions

1. R is a ring which is a finite-dimensional algebra over the rational number field $\mathbb{Q}$
2. $\mathcal{O}$ spans R over $\mathbb{Q}$, so that $\mathbb{Q}\mathcal{O} = R$, and
3. $\mathcal{O}$ is a lattice in R.

The third condition can be stated more accurately, in terms of the extension of scalars of R to the real numbers, embedding R in a real vector space. In less formal terms, additively $\mathcal{O}$ should be a free abelian group generated by a basis for R over $\mathbb{Q}$.

The leading example is the case where R is a number field K and $\mathcal{O}$ is its ring of integers. In algebraic number theory there are examples for any K other than the rational field of proper subrings of the ring of integers that are also _____s.

a. Annihilator
b. Algebraic
c. Efficiency
d. Order

40. In algebra and computer programming, when a number or expression is both preceded and followed by a binary operation, a rule is required for which operation should be applied first; this rule is known as an _____ . From the earliest use of mathematical notation, multiplication took precedence over addition, whichever side of a number it appeared on. Thus 3 + 4 × 5 = 5 × 4 + 3 = 23.

a. Isomorphism class
b. Algebraic K-theory
c. Order of operations
d. Identity element

41. In abstract algebra, a field extension L /K is called _____ if every element of L is _____ over K. Field extensions which are not _____.

For example, the field extension R/Q, that is the field of real numbers as an extension of the field of rational numbers, is transcendental, while the field extensions C/R and Q

a. Ideal
b. Algebraic
c. Echo
d. Identity

42. In mathematics, the multiplicative inverse of a number x, denoted 1/x or x^{-1}, is the number which, when multiplied by x, yields 1. The multiplicative inverse of x is also called the _____ of x.

a. 2-3 heap
c. 120-cell
b. 1-center problem
d. Reciprocal

43. In mathematics, the _____ or least common denominator is the least common multiple of the denominators of a set of vulgar fractions. It is the smallest positive integer that is a multiple of the denominators. For instance, the _____ of

$$\left\{\frac{5}{12}, \frac{11}{18}\right\}$$

is 36 because the least common multiple of 12 and 18 is 36.

a. Subtrahend
c. Highest common factor
b. The number 0 is even.
d. Lowest common denominator

44. The _____ of a material is defined as its mass per unit volume:

$$\rho = \frac{m}{V}$$

Different materials usually have different densities, so _____ is an important concept regarding buoyancy, metal purity and packaging.

In some cases _____ is expressed as the dimensionless quantities specific gravity or relative _____, in which case it is expressed in multiples of the _____ of some other standard material, usually water or air.

In a well-known story, Archimedes was given the task of determining whether King Hiero's goldsmith was embezzling gold during the manufacture of a wreath dedicated to the gods and replacing it with another, cheaper alloy.

a. 1-center problem
c. 2-3 heap
b. 120-cell
d. Density

45. In vascular plants, the _____ is the organ of a plant body that typically lies below the surface of the soil. This is not always the case, however, since a _____ can also be aerial (that is, growing above the ground) or aerating (that is, growing up above the ground or especially above water.) Furthermore, a stem normally occurring below ground is not exceptional either

a. 1-center problem
c. 2-3 heap
b. 120-cell
d. Root

46. In mathematics, an algebraic group G contains a unique maximal normal solvable subgroup; and this subgroup is closed. Its identity component is called the _____ of G.

a. Barycentric coordinates
c. Composite
b. Block size
d. Radical

Chapter 5. Number Theory and the Real Number System

47. In mathematics, a _____ of a number x is a number r such that r^2 = x, or, in other words, a number r whose square is x. Every non-negative real number x has a unique non-negative _____, called the principal _____, which is denoted with a radical symbol as $\sqrt{x}$, or, using exponent notation, as $x^{1/2}$. For example, the principal _____ of 9 is 3, denoted $\sqrt{9}$ = 3, because 3^2 = 3 × 3 = 9.
   a. Multiplicative inverse
   b. Hyperbolic functions
   c. Double exponential
   d. Square root

48. In geometry, a _____ is defined as a quadrilateral where all four of its angles are right angles.
   a. Point group in two dimensions
   b. Rectangle
   c. Cantor-Dedekind axiom
   d. Polytope

49. The _____ governs the differentiation of products of differentiable functions.
   a. 1-center problem
   b. Reciprocal Rule
   c. Product rule
   d. 120-cell

50. Exponentiation is a mathematical operation, written a^n, involving two numbers, the base a and the _____ n. When n is a positive integer, exponentiation corresponds to repeated multiplication:

$$a^n = \underbrace{a \times \cdots \times a}_{n},$$

just as multiplication by a positive integer corresponds to repeated addition:

$$a \times n = \underbrace{a + \cdots + a}_{n}.$$

The _____ is usually shown as a superscript to the right of the base. The exponentiation a^n can be read as: a raised to the n-th power, a raised to the power [of] n or possibly a raised to the _____ [of] n, or more briefly: a to the n-th power or a to the power [of] n, or even more briefly: a to the n.

   a. Exponential tree
   b. Exponential sum
   c. Exponentiating by squaring
   d. Exponent

51. In mathematics, a _____ is a constant multiplicative factor of a certain object. For example, in the expression $9x^2$, the _____ of x^2 is 9.

The object can be such things as a variable, a vector, a function, etc.

   a. Fibonacci polynomials
   b. Multivariate division algorithm
   c. Stability radius
   d. Coefficient

52. A _____ of a number is a number a such that a^3 = x.

a. Square root
b. Golden function
c. Hyperbolic functions
d. Cube root

53. In mathematics, the _____s may be described informally in several different ways. The _____s include both rational numbers, such as 42 and −23/129, and irrational numbers, such as pi and the square root of two; or, a _____ can be given by an infinite decimal representation, such as 2.4871773339...., where the digits continue in some way; or, the _____s may be thought of as points on an infinitely long number line.

These descriptions of the _____s, while intuitively accessible, are not sufficiently rigorous for the purposes of pure mathematics.

a. Pre-algebra
b. Minkowski distance
c. Tally marks
d. Real number

54. In mathematics, especially in set theory, a set A is a _____ of a set B if A is 'contained' inside B. Notice that A and B may coincide. The relationship of one set being a _____ of another is called inclusion.
a. Horizontal line test
b. Set of all sets
c. Cartesian product
d. Subset

55. _____ is an automatic theorem prover for first-order classical logic developed in the Computer Science Department of the University of Manchester by Prof. Andrei Voronkov previously together with Dr. Alexandre Riazanov. It has won the 'world cup for theorem provers' in the most prestigious CNF division for nine years.
a. Caesar cipher
b. Battleship
c. Polar coordinate
d. Vampire

56. In mathematics, a _____ is a natural number that is abundant but not semiperfect. In other words, the sum of the proper divisors of the number is greater than the number, but no subset of those divisors sums to the number itself.

The smallest _____ is 70.

a. Hofstadter sequence
b. Weird number
c. Regular paperfolding sequence
d. Carol number

57. In mathematics, a set is said to be _____ if the operation on members of the set produces a member of the set. For example, the real numbers are closed under subtraction, but the natural numbers are not: 3 and 7 are both natural numbers, but the result of 3 − 7 is not.

Similarly, a set is said to be closed under a collection of operations if it is closed under each of the operations individually.

a. Contingency table
b. Continuous linear extension
c. Control chart
d. Closed under some operation

58. The _____ is a rule which states that when you add or multiply numbers, changing the order doesn't change the result.

a. Coimage
b. Conditional event algebra
c. Semigroupoid
d. Commutative law

59. In mathematics, and in particular in abstract algebra, distributivity is a property of binary operations that generalises the _____ law from elementary algebra.
   a. Closure with a twist
   b. Permutation
   c. General linear group
   d. Distributive

60. In mathematics, a _____ (or true _____) is a composite natural number v, with an even number of digits n, that can be factored into two integers x and y each with n/2 digits and not both with trailing zeroes, where v contains all the digits from x and from y, in any order. x and y are called the fangs.

For example: 1260 is a _____, with 21 and 60 as fangs, since 21 × 60 = 1260.

   a. Frugal number
   b. Sum-product number
   c. Primeval number
   d. Vampire number

61. A _____ is a dynamic set of visual, auditory, or tactile symbols of communication and the elements used to manipulate them. _____ can also refer to the use of such systems as a general phenomenon. Strictly speaking, _____ is considered to be an exclusively human mode of communication.
   a. 1-center problem
   b. Language
   c. 2-3 heap
   d. 120-cell

62. A hypothesis consists either of a suggested explanation for an observable phenomenon or of a reasoned proposal predicting a possible causal correlation among multiple phenomena. The term derives from the Greek, hypotithenai meaning 'to put under' or 'to suppose.' The scientific method requires that one can test a scientific hypothesis. Scientists generally base such _____ on previous observations or on extensions of scientific theories.
   a. 2-3 heap
   b. 120-cell
   c. Hypotheses
   d. 1-center problem

63. In mathematics, an _____ is a complex number whose squared value is a real number less than or equal to zero. The imaginary unit, denoted by i or j, is an example of an _____. If y is a real number, then i·y is an _____, because:

$$(i \cdot y)^2 = i^2 \cdot y^2 = -y^2 \leq 0.$$

They were defined in 1572 by Rafael Bombelli.

   a. A posteriori
   b. A chemical equation
   c. A Mathematical Theory of Communication
   d. Imaginary number

64. In number theory, a _____ or pluperfect digital invariant (PPDI) or Armstrong number is a number that in a given base is the sum of its own digits to the power of the number of digits.

To put it algebraically, let $n = \sum_{i=1}^{k} d_i b^{i-1}$ be an integer with representation $d_k d_{k-1}...d_1$ in base-b notation. If $n = \sum_{i=1}^{k} d_i^k$ then n is a narcisstic number.

a. Truncatable prime
b. Repdigit
c. Narcissistic number
d. Kaprekar number

65. This article will state and prove the _____ for differentiation, and then use it to prove these two formulas.

The _____ for differentiation states that for every natural number n, the derivative of $f(x) = x^n$ is $f'(x) = nx^{n-1}$, that is,

$$(x^n)' = nx^{n-1}.$$

The _____ for integration

$$\int x^n \, dx = \frac{x^{n+1}}{n+1} + C$$

for natural n is then an easy consequence. One just needs to take the derivative of this equality and use the _____ and linearity of differentiation on the right-hand side.

a. Periodic function
b. Standard part function
c. Functional integration
d. Power Rule

66. A _____ is the large number 10^{100}, that is, the digit 1 followed by one hundred zeros. The term was coined in 1938 by Milton Sirotta, nephew of American mathematician Edward Kasner. Kasner popularized the concept in his book Mathematics and the Imagination.

a. 2-3 heap
b. 1-center problem
c. 120-cell
d. Googol

67. _____, also sometimes known as standard form or as exponential notation, is a way of writing numbers that accommodates values too large or small to be conveniently written in standard decimal notation. _____ has a number of useful properties and is often favored by scientists, mathematicians and engineers, who work with such numbers.

In _____, numbers are written in the form:

$$a \times 10^b$$

Chapter 5. Number Theory and the Real Number System 39

    a. 1-center problem
    b. Leading zero
    c. Radix point
    d. Scientific notation

68. _____ IPA: [pjɛːʁ dəˈmaʁ 'ma] (17 August 1601 or 1607/8 - 12 January 1665) was a French lawyer at the Parlement of Toulouse, France, and a mathematician who is given credit for early developments that led to modern calculus. In particular, he is recognized for his discovery of an original method of finding the greatest and the smallest ordinates of curved lines, which is analogous to that of the then unknown differential calculus, as well as his research into the theory of numbers. He also made notable contributions to analytic geometry, probability, and optics.
    a. Philip J. Davis
    b. Pierre de Fermat
    c. Felix Hausdorff
    d. Nikita Borisov

69. Leonardo of Pisa (c. 1170 - c. 1250), also known as Leonardo Pisano, Leonardo Bonacci, Leonardo _____, or, most commonly, simply _____, was an Italian mathematician, considered by some 'the most talented mathematician of the Middle Ages'.
    a. Guido Castelnuovo
    b. Ralph C. Merkle
    c. Harry Hinsley
    d. Fibonacci

70. In mathematics, a _____ is a curve which emanates from a central point, getting progressively farther away as it revolves around the point. An Archimedean _____, a helix, and a conic _____.

A '_____' and a 'helix' are two terms that are easily confused, but represent different objects.

A _____ is typically a planar curve, like the groove on a record or the arms of a _____ galaxy.

    a. Fresnel integrals
    b. Cornu spiral
    c. Logarithmic spiral
    d. Spiral

71. In mathematics, an arithmetic progression or _____ is a sequence of numbers such that the difference of any two successive members of the sequence is a constant. For instance, the sequence 3, 5, 7, 9, 11, 13... is an arithmetic progression with common difference 2.
    a. Alternating series test
    b. Eisenstein series
    c. Edgeworth series
    d. Arithmetic sequence

72. _____ is the change in population over time, and can be quantified as the change in the number of individuals in a population using 'per unit time' for measurement. The term _____ can technically refer to any species, but almost always refers to humans, and it is often used informally for the more specific demographic term _____ rate, and is often used to refer specifically to the growth of the population of the world.

Simple models of _____ include the Malthusian Growth Model and the logistic model.

    a. Population dynamics
    b. 120-cell
    c. 1-center problem
    d. Population growth

Chapter 6. Algebra: Equations and Inequalities

1. In abstract algebra, a field extension L /K is called _____ if every element of L is _____ over K. Field extensions which are not _____.

   For example, the field extension R/Q, that is the field of real numbers as an extension of the field of rational numbers, is transcendental, while the field extensions C/R and Q

   a. Ideal
   b. Echo
   c. Identity
   d. Algebraic

2. In mathematics, an _____ in the sense of ring theory is a subring $\mathcal{O}$ of a ring R that satisfies the conditions

   1. R is a ring which is a finite-dimensional algebra over the rational number field $\mathbb{Q}$
   2. $\mathcal{O}$ spans R over $\mathbb{Q}$, so that $\mathbb{Q}\mathcal{O} = R$, and
   3. $\mathcal{O}$ is a lattice in R.

   The third condition can be stated more accurately, in terms of the extension of scalars of R to the real numbers, embedding R in a real vector space. In less formal terms, additively $\mathcal{O}$ should be a free abelian group generated by a basis for R over $\mathbb{Q}$.

   The leading example is the case where R is a number field K and $\mathcal{O}$ is its ring of integers. In algebraic number theory there are examples for any K other than the rational field of proper subrings of the ring of integers that are also _____ s.

   a. Annihilator
   b. Efficiency
   c. Algebraic
   d. Order

3. In algebra and computer programming, when a number or expression is both preceded and followed by a binary operation, a rule is required for which operation should be applied first; this rule is known as an _____ . From the earliest use of mathematical notation, multiplication took precedence over addition, whichever side of a number it appeared on. Thus 3 + 4 × 5 = 5 × 4 + 3 = 23.

   a. Order of operations
   b. Isomorphism class
   c. Identity element
   d. Algebraic K-theory

4. In mathematics and in the sciences, a _____ (plural: _____ e, formulæ or _____ s) is a concise way of expressing information symbolically (as in a mathematical or chemical _____), or a general relationship between quantities. One of many famous _____ e is Albert Einstein's $E = mc^2$ (see special relativity

   In mathematics, a _____ is a key to solve an equation with variables. For example, the problem of determining the volume of a sphere is one that requires a significant amount of integral calculus to solve.

   a. 2-3 heap
   b. 1-center problem
   c. 120-cell
   d. Formula

5. A _____ is an abstract model that uses mathematical language to describe the behavior of a system. Eykhoff defined a _____ as 'a representation of the essential aspects of an existing system which presents knowledge of that system in usable form'.

Chapter 6. Algebra: Equations and Inequalities 41

   a. Rata Die
   b. Mathematical model
   c. Total least squares
   d. Metaheuristic

6. In ecology, predation describes a biological interaction where a _____ (an organism that is hunting) feeds on its prey, the organism that is attacked. _____s may or may not kill their prey prior to feeding on them, but the act of predation always results in the death of the prey. The other main category of consumption is detritivory, the consumption of dead organic material (detritus.)
   a. Prey
   b. 120-cell
   c. 1-center problem
   d. Predator

7. In mathematics, _____ is a property that a binary operation can have. It means that, within an expression containing two or more of the same associative operators in a row, the order that the operations are performed does not matter as long as the sequence of the operands is not changed. That is, rearranging the parentheses in such an expression will not change its value.
   a. Algebraically closed
   b. Idempotence
   c. Associativity
   d. Unital

8. In mathematics, a _____ is a constant multiplicative factor of a certain object. For example, in the expression $9x^2$, the _____ of x^2 is 9.

The object can be such things as a variable, a vector, a function, etc.

   a. Fibonacci polynomials
   b. Multivariate division algorithm
   c. Stability radius
   d. Coefficient

9. The _____ is a rule which states that when you add or multiply numbers, changing the order doesn't change the result.
   a. Conditional event algebra
   b. Coimage
   c. Commutative law
   d. Semigroupoid

10. In mathematics, and in particular in abstract algebra, distributivity is a property of binary operations that generalises the _____ law from elementary algebra.
   a. Distributive
   b. Closure with a twist
   c. Permutation
   d. General linear group

11. In mathematics, the _____s may be described informally in several different ways. The _____s include both rational numbers, such as 42 and −23/129, and irrational numbers, such as pi and the square root of two; or, a _____ can be given by an infinite decimal representation, such as 2.4871773339...., where the digits continue in some way; or, the _____s may be thought of as points on an infinitely long number line.

These descriptions of the _____s, while intuitively accessible, are not sufficiently rigorous for the purposes of pure mathematics.

   a. Real number
   b. Tally marks
   c. Pre-algebra
   d. Minkowski distance

Chapter 6. Algebra: Equations and Inequalities

12. _____ is the mathematical operation of scaling one number by another. It is one of the four basic operations in elementary arithmetic.

_____ is defined for whole numbers in terms of repeated addition; for example, 4 multiplied by 3 can be calculated by adding 3 copies of 4 together:

$$4 + 4 + 4 = 12.$$

_____ of rational numbers and real numbers is defined by systematic generalization of this basic idea.

   a. Highest common factor
   c. The number 0 is even.
   b. Least common multiple
   d. Multiplication

13. A _____ is an algebraic equation in which each term is either a constant or the product of a constant and a single variable. _____s can have one, two, three or more variables.

_____s occur with great regularity in applied mathematics.

   a. Quadratic equation
   c. Difference of two squares
   b. Quartic equation
   d. Linear equation

14. In mathematics, _____ and undefined are used to explain whether or not expressions have meaningful, sensible, and unambiguous values. Not all branches of mathematics come to the same conclusion.

The following expressions are undefined in all contexts, but remarks in the analysis section may apply.

   a. Toy model
   c. LHS
   b. Plugging in
   d. Defined

15. In the study of metric spaces in mathematics, there are various notions of two metrics on the same underlying space being 'the same', or _____.

In the following, M will denote a non-empty set and d_1 and d_2 will denote two metrics on M.

The two metrics d_1 and d_2 are said to be topologically _____ if they generate the same topology on M.

   a. Equivalent
   c. A Mathematical Theory of Communication
   b. A chemical equation
   d. A posteriori

16. In mathematics, the _____ or least common denominator is the least common multiple of the denominators of a set of vulgar fractions. It is the smallest positive integer that is a multiple of the denominators. For instance, the _____ of

$$\left\{\frac{5}{12}, \frac{11}{18}\right\}$$

is 36 because the least common multiple of 12 and 18 is 36.

a. Highest common factor
b. The number 0 is even.
c. Subtrahend
d. Lowest common denominator

17. _____ or set diagrams are diagrams that show all hypothetically possible logical relations between a finite collection of sets. _____ were invented around 1880 by John Venn. They are used in many fields, including set theory, probability, logic, statistics, and computer science.
a. 1-center problem
b. 120-cell
c. 2-3 heap
d. Venn diagrams

18. A _____ is a 2D geometric symbolic representation of information according to some visualization technique. Sometimes, the technique uses a 3D visualization which is then projected onto the 2D surface. The word graph is sometimes used as a synonym for _____.
a. Diagram
b. 2-3 heap
c. 1-center problem
d. 120-cell

19. A _____ is a software program that facilitates symbolic mathematics. The core functionality of a CAS is manipulation of mathematical expressions in symbolic form.

The symbolic manipulations supported typically include

- simplification to the smallest possible expression or some standard form, including automatic simplification with assumptions and simplification with constraints
- substitution of symbolic, functors or numeric values for expressions
- change of form of expressions: expanding products and powers, partial and full factorization, rewriting as partial fractions, constraint satisfaction, rewriting trigonometric functions as exponentials, etc.
- partial and total differentiation
- symbolic constrained and unconstrained global optimization
- solution of linear and some non-linear equations over various domains
- solution of some differential and difference equations
- taking some limits
- some indefinite and definite integration, including multidimensional integrals
- integral transforms
- arbitrary-precision numeric operations
- Series operations such as expansion, summation and products
- matrix operations including products, inverses, etc.
- display of mathematical expressions in two-dimensional mathematical form, often using typesetting systems similar to TeX
- add-ons for use in applied mathematics such as physics packages for physical computation
- plotting graphs and parametric plots of functions in two and three dimensions, and animating them
- APIs for linking it on an external program such as a database, or using in a programming language to use the _____
- drawing charts and diagrams
- string manipulation such as matching and searching
- statistical computation
- Theorem proving and verification
- graphic production and editing such as CGI and signal processing as image processing
- sound synthesis

Many also include a programming language, allowing users to implement their own algorithms.

Some _____s focus on a specific area of application; these are typically developed in academia and are free.

a. 1-center problem
b. 120-cell
c. 2-3 heap
d. Computer algebra system

20. In mathematics, especially in the area of abstract algebra known as combinatorial group theory, the _____ for a recursively presented group G is the algorithmic problem of deciding whether two words represent the same element. Although it is common to speak of the _____ for the group G strictly speaking it is a presentation of the group that does or does not have solvable _____. Given two finite presentations P and Q of a group G, P has solvable _____ if and only if Q does.

Chapter 6. Algebra: Equations and Inequalities

   a. Prime ideal theorem
   b. Torsion
   c. Computational mathematics
   d. Word problem

21. In game theory, a player's _____ in a game is a complete plan of action for whatever situation might arise; this fully determines the player's behaviour. A player's _____ will determine the action the player will take at any stage of the game, for every possible history of play up to that stage.

A _____ profile is a set of strategies for each player which fully specifies all actions in a game.

   a. Matching pennies
   b. Strategy
   c. Sir Philip Sidney game
   d. Correlated equilibrium

22. _____ is the interpreting of the meaning of a text and the subsequent production of an equivalent text, likewise called a '_____,' that communicates the same message in another language. The text to be translated is called the 'source text,' and the language that it is to be translated into is called the 'target language'; the final product is sometimes called the 'target text.'

_____ must take into account constraints that include context, the rules of grammar of the two languages, their writing conventions, and their idioms. A common misconception is that there exists a simple word-for-word correspondence between any two languages, and that _____ is a straightforward mechanical process; such a word-for-word _____, however, cannot take into account context, grammar, conventions, and idioms.

   a. 120-cell
   b. 2-3 heap
   c. 1-center problem
   d. Translation

23. _____ is a special mathematical relationship between two quantities. Two quantities are called proportional if they vary in such a way that one of the quantities is a constant multiple of the other, or equivalently if they have a constant ratio.
   a. Depth
   b. Compression
   c. Proportionality
   d. Discontinuity

24. In signal processing, _____ is the reduction of a continuous signal to a discrete signal. A common example is the conversion of a sound wave to a sequence of samples.

A sample refers to a value or set of values at a point in time and/or space.

   a. Converse logic
   b. Sampling
   c. Decidable
   d. Disk

25. In mathematics, the _____ of a number n is the number that, when added to n, yields zero. The _____ of n is denoted −n. For example, 7 is −7, because 7 + (−7) = 0, and the _____ of −0.3 is 0.3, because −0.3 + 0.3 = 0.
   a. Associativity
   b. Algebraic structure
   c. Arity
   d. Additive inverse

26. In geometry and trigonometry, an _____ is the figure formed by two rays sharing a common endpoint, called the vertex of the _____. The magnitude of the _____ is the 'amount of rotation' that separates the two rays, and can be measured by considering the length of circular arc swept out when one ray is rotated about the vertex to coincide with the other. Where there is no possibility of confusion, the term '_____' is used interchangeably for both the geometric configuration itself and for its angular magnitude.

   a. A chemical equation   b. A Mathematical Theory of Communication
   c. A posteriori   d. Angle

27. In mathematics, an _____ is a statement about the relative size or order of two objects, or about whether they are the same or not

- The notation a < b means that a is less than b.
- The notation a > b means that a is greater than b.
- The notation a ≠ b means that a is not equal to b, but does not say that one is bigger than the other or even that they can be compared in size.

In all these cases, a is not equal to b, hence, '_____'.

These relations are known as strict _____

- The notation a ≤ b means that a is less than or equal to b;
- The notation a ≥ b means that a is greater than or equal to b;

An additional use of the notation is to show that one quantity is much greater than another, normally by several orders of magnitude.

- The notation a << b means that a is much less than b.
- The notation a >> b means that a is much greater than b.

If the sense of the _____ is the same for all values of the variables for which its members are defined, then the _____ is called an 'absolute' or 'unconditional' _____. If the sense of an _____ holds only for certain values of the variables involved, but is reversed or destroyed for other values of the variables, it is called a conditional _____.

An _____ may appear unsolvable because it only states whether a number is larger or smaller than another number; but it is possible to apply the same operations for equalities to inequalities. For example, to find x for the _____ 10x > 23 one would divide 23 by 10.

   a. A chemical equation   b. A Mathematical Theory of Communication
   c. A posteriori   d. Inequality

28. In mathematics, a _____ is a picture of a straight line in which the integers are shown as specially-marked points evenly spaced on the line. Although this image only shows the integers from -9 to 9, the line includes all real numbers, continuing 'forever' in each direction. It is often used as an aid in teaching simple addition and subtraction, especially involving negative numbers.

Chapter 6. Algebra: Equations and Inequalities

47

    a. Point plotting
    c. Real number
    b. Number line
    d. Number system

29. In mathematics, especially in set theory, a set A is a _____ of a set B if A is 'contained' inside B. Notice that A and B may coincide. The relationship of one set being a _____ of another is called inclusion.
    a. Cartesian product
    c. Horizontal line test
    b. Set of all sets
    d. Subset

30. In graph theory, a _____ in a graph is a sequence of vertices such that from each of its vertices there is an edge to the next vertex in the sequence. The first vertex is called the start vertex and the last vertex is called the end vertex. Both of them are called end or terminal vertices of the _____.
    a. Deltoid
    c. Blinding
    b. Class
    d. Path

31. In elementary algebra, a _____ is a polynomial with two terms: the sum of two monomials. It is the simplest kind of polynomial except for a monomial.

The _____ $a^2 - b^2$ can be factored as the product of two other _____s:

$a^2 - b^2$.

The product of a pair of linear _____s $ax + b$ and $cx + d$ is:

$2 + x + bd$.

A _____ raised to the nth power, represented as

n

can be expanded by means of the _____ theorem or, equivalently, using Pascal's triangle.

    a. Rational root theorem
    c. Cylindrical algebraic decomposition
    b. Binomial
    d. Real structure

32. In mathematics, a _____ is a polynomial equation of the second degree. The general form is

$$ax^2 + bx + c = 0,$$

where $a \neq 0$.

The letters a, b, and c are called coefficients: the quadratic coefficient a is the coefficient of x^2, the linear coefficient b is the coefficient of x, and c is the constant coefficient, also called the free term or constant term.

a. Difference of two squares
b. Quadratic equation
c. Quartic equation
d. Linear equation

33. In linear algebra, two n-by-n matrices A and B over the field K are called _____ if there exists an invertible n-by-n matrix P over K such that

$$P^{-1}AP = B.$$

One of the meanings of the term similarity transformation is such a transformation of a matrix A into a matrix B.

Similarity is an equivalence relation on the space of square matrices.

_____ matrices share many properties:

- rank
- determinant
- trace
- eigenvalues
- characteristic polynomial
- minimal polynomial
- elementary divisors

There are two reasons for these facts:

- two _____ matrices can be thought of as describing the same linear map, but with respect to different bases
- the map $X \mapsto P^{-1}XP$ is an automorphism of the associative algebra of all n-by-n matrices, as the one-object case of the above category of all matrices.

Because of this, for a given matrix A, one is interested in finding a simple 'normal form' B which is _____ to A -- the study of A then reduces to the study of the simpler matrix B.

a. Dense
b. Similar
c. Coherence
d. Blinding

34. A _____ is one of the basic shapes of geometry: a polygon with three corners or vertices and three sides or edges which are line segments. A _____ with vertices A, B, and C is denoted ABC.

In Euclidean geometry any three non-collinear points determine a unique _____ and a unique plane.

a. Fuhrmann circle
b. 1-center problem
c. Kepler triangle
d. Triangle

Chapter 6. Algebra: Equations and Inequalities

35. In mathematics, a _____ is an expression constructed from variables and constants, using the operations of addition, subtraction, multiplication, and constant non-negative whole number exponents. For example, $x^2 - 4x + 7$ is a _____, but $x^2 - 4/x + 7x^{3/2}$ is not, because its second term involves division by the variable x and also because its third term contains an exponent that is not a whole number.

_____s are one of the most important concepts in algebra and throughout mathematics and science.

a. Semifield
c. Group extension
b. Coimage
d. Polynomial

36. In elementary algebra, a _____ is a polynomial consisting of three terms; in other words, a _____ is the sum of three monomials. It can be factored using simple steps

In linguistics, a _____ is a fixed expression which is made from three words; e.g. 'lights, camera, action', 'signed, sealed, delivered'.

a. Recurrence relation
c. Relation algebra
b. Symmetric difference
d. Trinomial

37. In mathematics, a _____ is a natural number which has exactly two distinct natural number divisors: 1 and itself. An infinitude of _____s exists, as demonstrated by Euclid around 300 BC. The first twenty-five _____s are:

2, 3, 5, 7, 11, 13, 17, 19, 23, 29, 31, 37, 41, 43, 47, 53, 59, 61, 67, 71, 73, 79, 83, 89, 97.

a. Perrin number
c. Pronic number
b. Prime number
d. Highly composite number

38. A quadratic equation with real solutions, called roots, which may be real or complex, is given by the _____: $x = \frac{-b \pm \sqrt{b^2 - 4ac}}{2a}$.

a. Parametric continuity
c. Differential Algebra
b. Quotient
d. Quadratic formula

39. In mathematics, an _____ is a complex number whose squared value is a real number less than or equal to zero. The imaginary unit, denoted by i or j, is an example of an _____. If y is a real number, then i·y is an _____, because:

$$(i \cdot y)^2 = i^2 \cdot y^2 = -y^2 \leq 0.$$

They were defined in 1572 by Rafael Bombelli.

a. A Mathematical Theory of Communication
c. A posteriori
b. Imaginary number
d. A chemical equation

Chapter 6. Algebra: Equations and Inequalities

40. A _____ typically refers to a class of handheld calculators that are capable of plotting graphs, solving simultaneous equations, and performing numerous other tasks with variables. Most popular _____s are also programmable, allowing the user to create customized programs, typically for scientific/engineering and education applications. Due to their large displays intended for graphing, they can also accommodate several lines of text and calculations at a time.
   a. Genus
   b. Bump mapping
   c. Support vector machines
   d. Graphing calculator

41. A _____ is a device for performing mathematical calculations, distinguished from a computer by having a limited problem solving ability and an interface optimized for interactive calculation rather than programming. _____s can be hardware or software, and mechanical or electronic, and are often built into devices such as PDAs or mobile phones.

   Modern electronic _____s are generally small, digital, and usually inexpensive.

   a. Calculator
   b. 2-3 heap
   c. 120-cell
   d. 1-center problem

42. The _____ are the set of numbers consisting of the natural numbers including 0 and their negatives. They are numbers that can be written without a fractional or decimal component, and fall within the set {... −2, −1, 0, 1, 2, ...}.
   a. A chemical equation
   b. Integers
   c. A posteriori
   d. A Mathematical Theory of Communication

Chapter 7. Algebra: Graphs, Functions, and Linear Systems　　　　　　　　　　　　　　51

1. _____ is the study of geometry using the principles of algebra. That the algebra of the real numbers can be employed to yield results about the linear continuum of geometry relies on the Cantor-Dedekind axiom. Usually the Cartesian coordinate system is applied to manipulate equations for planes, straight lines, and squares, often in two and sometimes in three dimensions of measurement.

   a. Angular eccentricity
   b. Axis-aligned object
   c. Ambient space
   d. Analytic geometry

2. _____ IPA: [pjɛʁ ɛ dɛ™fɛʁ 'ma] (17 August 1601 or 1607/8 - 12 January 1665) was a French lawyer at the Parlement of Toulouse, France, and a mathematician who is given credit for early developments that led to modern calculus. In particular, he is recognized for his discovery of an original method of finding the greatest and the smallest ordinates of curved lines, which is analogous to that of the then unknown differential calculus, as well as his research into the theory of numbers. He also made notable contributions to analytic geometry, probability, and optics.

   a. Pierre de Fermat
   b. Philip J. Davis
   c. Felix Hausdorff
   d. Nikita Borisov

3. _____ Galilei (15 February 1564 - 8 January 1642) was a Tuscan physicist, mathematician, astronomer, and philosopher who played a major role in the Scientific Revolution. His achievements include improvements to the telescope and consequent astronomical observations, and support for Copernicanism. _____ has been called the 'father of modern observational astronomy', the 'father of modern physics', the 'father of science', and 'the Father of Modern Science.' The motion of uniformly accelerated objects, taught in nearly all high school and introductory college physics courses, was studied by _____ as the subject of kinematics.

   a. David Naccache
   b. Francesco Severi
   c. Galileo
   d. Jan Kowalewski

4. _____ is a part of mathematics concerned with questions of size, shape, and relative position of figures and with properties of space. _____ is one of the oldest sciences. Initially a body of practical knowledge concerning lengths, areas, and volumes, in the third century BC _____ was put into an axiomatic form by Euclid, whose treatment--Euclidean _____--set a standard for many centuries to follow.

   a. 2-3 heap
   b. Geometry
   c. 1-center problem
   d. 120-cell

5. _____ is the likelihood or chance that something is the case or will happen. Theoretical _____ is used extensively in areas such as statistics, mathematics, science and philosophy to draw conclusions about the likelihood of potential events and the underlying mechanics of complex systems.

The word _____ does not have a consistent direct definition.

   a. Standardized moment
   b. Statistical significance
   c. Probability
   d. Discrete random variable

6. _____ is the branch of mathematics concerned with analysis of random phenomena. The central objects of _____ are random variables, stochastic processes, and events: mathematical abstractions of non-deterministic events or measured quantities that may either be single occurrences or evolve over time in an apparently random fashion. Although an individual coin toss or the roll of a die is a random event, if repeated many times the sequence of random events will exhibit certain statistical patterns, which can be studied and predicted.

a. Law of large numbers
b. Probability theory
c. Standard probability space
d. Martingale central limit theorem

7. In mathematics, the _____ or Pythagoras' theorem is a relation in Euclidean geometry among the three sides of a right triangle. The theorem is named after the Greek mathematician Pythagoras, who by tradition is credited with its discovery and proof, although it is often argued that knowledge of the theory predates him.. The theorem is as follows:

In any right triangle, the area of the square whose side is the hypotenuse is equal to the sum of the areas of the squares whose sides are the two legs.

a. 2-3 heap
b. Pythagorean Theorem
c. 1-center problem
d. 120-cell

8. A _____ consists of one quarter of the coordinate plane.
a. 120-cell
b. Quadrant
c. 2-3 heap
d. 1-center problem

9. In mathematics, a _____ is a statement that can be proved on the basis of explicitly stated or previously agreed assumptions.
a. Boolean function
b. Theorem
c. Disjunction introduction
d. Logical value

10. The word _____ has many distinct meanings in different fields of knowledge, depending on their methodologies and the context of discussion. Broadly speaking we can say that a _____ is some kind of belief or claim that (supposedly) explains, asserts, or consolidates some class of claims. Additionally, in contrast with a theorem the statement of the _____ is generally accepted only in some tentative fashion as opposed to regarding it as having been conclusively established.
a. Per mil
b. Transport of structure
c. Defined
d. Theory

11. The _____ is the horizontal axis of a two- dimensional plot in the Cartesian coordinate system, that is typically pointed to the right. Also known as a right-handed coordinate system.
a. 2-3 heap
b. 1-center problem
c. 120-cell
d. X-axis

12. The _____ is one of the coordinates of a point in a two or three-dimensional cartesian coordinate system, equal to the distance of a point from the y-axis in a 2D system, or from the plane of y and z axes in a 3D system, measured along a line parallel to the x axis.
a. 120-cell
b. X-coordinate
c. 2-3 heap
d. 1-center problem

13. In reference to a 2D and 3D plane, the _____ is the vertical height of a 2D or 3D object.
a. 120-cell
b. 1-center problem
c. 2-3 heap
d. Y-axis

Chapter 7. Algebra: Graphs, Functions, and Linear Systems

14. The mathematical concept of a _____ expresses the intuitive idea of deterministic dependence between two quantities, one of which is viewed as primary and the other as secondary. A _____ then is a way to associate a unique output for each input of a specified type, for example, a real number or an element of a given set.
    a. Going up
    b. Function
    c. Coherent
    d. Grill

15. In mathematics, _____ and undefined are used to explain whether or not expressions have meaningful, sensible, and unambiguous values. Not all branches of mathematics come to the same conclusion.

    The following expressions are undefined in all contexts, but remarks in the analysis section may apply.

    a. LHS
    b. Plugging in
    c. Toy model
    d. Defined

16. A _____ typically refers to a class of handheld calculators that are capable of plotting graphs, solving simultaneous equations, and performing numerous other tasks with variables. Most popular _____ s are also programmable, allowing the user to create customized programs, typically for scientific/engineering and education applications. Due to their large displays intended for graphing, they can also accommodate several lines of text and calculations at a time.
    a. Bump mapping
    b. Graphing calculator
    c. Genus
    d. Support vector machines

17. A _____ is a device for performing mathematical calculations, distinguished from a computer by having a limited problem solving ability and an interface optimized for interactive calculation rather than programming. _____ s can be hardware or software, and mechanical or electronic, and are often built into devices such as PDAs or mobile phones.

    Modern electronic _____ s are generally small, digital, and usually inexpensive.

    a. 120-cell
    b. 2-3 heap
    c. 1-center problem
    d. Calculator

18. The _____ are the set of numbers consisting of the natural numbers including 0 and their negatives. They are numbers that can be written without a fractional or decimal component, and fall within the set {... −2, −1, 0, 1, 2, ...}.
    a. Integers
    b. A Mathematical Theory of Communication
    c. A posteriori
    d. A chemical equation

19. To define the derivative of a distribution, we first consider the case of a differentiable and integrable function f : R → R. If φ is a _____, then we have

$$\int_R f'\varphi \, dx = -\int_R f\varphi' \, dx$$

using integration by parts (note that φ is zero outside of a bounded set and that therefore no boundary values have to be taken into account.) This suggests that if S is a distribution, we should define its derivative S' by

$$\langle S', \varphi \rangle = - \langle S, \varphi' \rangle$$

a. Schwartz kernel theorem
b. Test Function
c. Hyperfunction
d. Generalized functions

20. A _____ is an opening in a wall that allows the passage of light and, if not closed or sealed, air and sound. _____s are usually glazed or covered in some other transparent or translucent material. _____s are held in place by frames, which prevent them from collapsing in.

a. Window
b. 120-cell
c. 1-center problem
d. 2-3 heap

21. A _____ is an algebraic equation in which each term is either a constant or the product of a constant and a single variable. _____s can have one, two, three or more variables.

_____s occur with great regularity in applied mathematics.

a. Quartic equation
b. Difference of two squares
c. Quadratic equation
d. Linear equation

22. In graph theory, a _____ in a graph is a sequence of vertices such that from each of its vertices there is an edge to the next vertex in the sequence. The first vertex is called the start vertex and the last vertex is called the end vertex. Both of them are called end or terminal vertices of the _____.

a. Class
b. Deltoid
c. Path
d. Blinding

23. _____ is used to describe the steepness, incline, gradient, or grade of a straight line. A higher _____ value indicates a steeper incline. The _____ is defined as the ratio of the 'rise' divided by the 'run' between two points on a line, or in other words, the ratio of the altitude change to the horizontal distance between any two points on the line.

a. Cognitively Guided Instruction
b. Slope
c. Number line
d. Point plotting

24. _____ is a form where m is the slope of the line and b is the y-intercept, which is the y-coordinate of the point where the line crosses the y axis. This can be seen by letting x = 0, which immediately gives y = b.

a. Dynamical system
b. Commutative law
c. Slope-intercept form
d. Separable extension

25. In mathematics, the _____ is an approach to finding a particular solution to certain inhomogeneous ordinary differential equations and recurrence relations. It is closely related to the annihilator method, but instead of using a particular kind of differential operator in order to find the best possible form of the particular solution, a 'guess' is made as to the appropriate form, which is then tested by differentiating the resulting equation. In this sense, the _____ is less formal but more intuitive than the annihilator method.

a. Method of undetermined coefficients
b. Phase line
c. Differential algebraic equations
d. Linear differential equation

26. In trigonometry, the _____ is a function defined as tan x = sin x / cos x. The function is so-named because it can be defined as the length of a certain segment of a _____ (in the geometric sense) to the unit circle. In plane geometry, a line is _____ to a curve, at some point, if both line and curve pass through the point with the same direction.
a. Hopf conjectures
b. Projective connection
c. Conformal geometry
d. Tangent

27. In combinatorial mathematics, a _____ is an un-ordered collection of distinct elements, usually of a prescribed size and taken from a given set. Given such a set S, a _____ of elements of S is just a subset of S, where as always forsets the order of the elements is not taken into account. Also, as always forsets, no elements can be repeated more than once in a _____; this is often referred to as a 'collection without repetition'.
a. Sparsity
b. Fill-in
c. Combination
d. Heawood number

28. A _____ is a mathematical model of a system based on the use of a linear operator. _____s typically exhibit features and properties that are much simpler than the general, nonlinear case. As a mathematical abstraction or idealization, _____s find important applications in automatic control theory, signal processing, and telecommunications.
a. Percolation
b. Predispositioning Theory
c. Hybrid system
d. Linear system

29. In mathematics, a _____ is a collection of linear equations involving the same set of variables. For example,

$$3x + 2y - z = 1$$
$$2x - 2y + 4z = -2$$
$$-x + \tfrac{1}{2}y - z = 0$$

is a system of three equations in the three variables x, y, z. A solution to a linear system is an assignment of numbers to the variables such that all the equations are simultaneously satisfied.

a. Hypsometric equation
b. Quintic equation
c. Slutsky equation
d. System of linear equations

30. In economics, specifically cost accounting, the _____ is the point at which cost or expenses and revenue are equal: there is no net loss or gain, and one has 'broken even'. Therefore has not made a profit or a loss.

In the linear Cost-Volume-Profit Analysis model, the _____ can be directly computed in terms of Total Revenue and Total Costs as:

$$TR = TC$$
$$P \times X = TFC + V \times X$$
$$P \times X - V \times X = TFC$$
$$(P - V) \times X = TFC$$
$$X = \frac{TFC}{P - V}$$

where:

- TFC is Total Fixed Costs,
- P is Unit Sale Price, and
- V is Unit Variable Cost.

The _____ can alternatively be computed as the point where Contribution equals Fixed Costs.

The quantity $(P - V)$ is of interest in its own right, and is called the Unit Contribution Margin: it is the marginal profit per unit, or alternatively the portion of each sale that contributes to Fixed Costs. Thus the _____ can be more simply computed as the point where Total Contribution = Total Fixed Cost:

$$\text{Total Contribution} = \text{Total Fixed Costs}$$
$$\text{Unit Contribution} \times \text{Number of Units} = \text{Total Fixed Costs}$$
$$\text{Number of Units} = \frac{\text{Total Fixed Costs}}{\text{Unit Contribution}}$$

In currency units to reach break-even, one can use the above calculation and multiply by Price, or equivalently use the Contribution Margin Ratio to compute it as:

$$\text{Break-even(in Sales)} = \frac{\text{Fixed Costs}}{C/P}.$$

R=C Where R is revenue generated C is cost incurred.

a. 120-cell
c. Small numbers game

b. 1-center problem
d. Break-even point

31. In economics, business, retail, and accounting, a _____ is the value of money that has been used up to produce something, and hence is not available for use anymore. In business, the _____ may be one of acquisition, in which case the amount of money expended to acquire it is counted as _____. In this case, money is the input that is gone in order to acquire the thing.

a. 2-3 heap
c. 120-cell

b. 1-center problem
d. Cost

32. In economics, the cross elasticity of demand and _____ measures the responsiveness of the quantity demanded of a good to a change in the price of another good.

It is measured as the percentage change in quantity demanded for the first good that occurs in response to a percentage change in price of the second good. For example, if, in response to a 10% increase in the price of fuel, the quantity of new cars that are fuel inefficient demanded decreased by 20%, the cross elasticity of demand would be -20%/10% = -2.

a. Supply and demand
b. 1-center problem
c. Cross price elasticity of demand
d. Marginal rate of substitution

33. _____ is a general term for any type of information processing. This includes phenomena ranging from human thinking to calculations with a more narrow meaning. _____ is a process following a well-defined model that is understood and can be expressed in an algorithm, protocol, network topology, etc.
a. 120-cell
b. 1-center problem
c. 2-3 heap
d. Computation

34. In mathematics, an _____ is a statement about the relative size or order of two objects, or about whether they are the same or not

- The notation a < b means that a is less than b.
- The notation a > b means that a is greater than b.
- The notation a ≠ b means that a is not equal to b, but does not say that one is bigger than the other or even that they can be compared in size.

In all these cases, a is not equal to b, hence, '_____'.

These relations are known as strict _____

- The notation a ≤ b means that a is less than or equal to b;
- The notation a ≥ b means that a is greater than or equal to b;

An additional use of the notation is to show that one quantity is much greater than another, normally by several orders of magnitude.

- The notation a << b means that a is much less than b.
- The notation a >> b means that a is much greater than b.

If the sense of the _____ is the same for all values of the variables for which its members are defined, then the _____ is called an 'absolute' or 'unconditional' _____. If the sense of an _____ holds only for certain values of the variables involved, but is reversed or destroyed for other values of the variables, it is called a conditional _____.

An _____ may appear unsolvable because it only states whether a number is larger or smaller than another number; but it is possible to apply the same operations for equalities to inequalities. For example, to find x for the _____ 10x > 23 one would divide 23 by 10.

a. A posteriori
b. A chemical equation
c. Inequality
d. A Mathematical Theory of Communication

35. _____ is either of the two parts into which a plane divides the three-dimensional space. More generally, a _____ is either of the two parts into which a hyperplane divides an affine space.

a. Parallelogram law
c. Pendent
b. Simple polytope
d. Half-space

36. In mathematics, _____ is a technique for optimization of a linear objective function, subject to linear equality and linear inequality constraints. Informally, _____ determines the way to achieve the best outcome in a given mathematical model given some list of requirements represented as linear equations.

More formally, given a polytope, and a real-valued affine function

$$f(x_1, x_2, \ldots, x_n) = c_1 x_1 + c_2 x_2 + \cdots + c_n x_n + d$$

defined on this polytope, a _____ method will find a point in the polytope where this function has the smallest value.

a. Lin-Kernighan
c. Descent direction
b. Linear programming relaxation
d. Linear programming

37. An _____ is a tree data structure in which each internal node has up to eight children. _____s are most often used to partition a three dimensional space by recursively subdividing it into eight octants. _____s are the three-dimensional analog of quadtrees.

a. Adaptive k-d tree
c. Interval tree
b. External node
d. Octree

38. In mathematics, a _____ is a condition that a solution to an optimization problem must satisfy. There are two types of _____s: equality _____s and inequality _____s. The set of solutions that satisfy all _____s is called the feasible set.

a. Decidable
c. Foci
b. Constraint
d. Concurrent

39. In probability theory and statistics, _____ indicates the strength and direction of a linear relationship between two random variables. That is in contrast with the usage of the term in colloquial speech, denoting any relationship, not necessarily linear. In general statistical usage, _____ or co-relation refers to the departure of two random variables from independence.

a. Summary statistics
c. Sample size
b. Correlation
d. Random variables

40. The _____ is a function in mathematics. The application of this function to a value x is written as ex. Equivalently, this can be written in the form e^x, where e is a mathematical constant, the base of the natural logarithm, which equals approximately 2.718281828, and is also known as Euler's number.

a. Area hyperbolic functions
c. A Mathematical Theory of Communication
b. A chemical equation
d. Exponential function

Chapter 7. Algebra: Graphs, Functions, and Linear Systems

41. In mathematics, a _____ is a system which is not linear. Less technically, a _____ is any problem where the variabl to be solved for cannot be written as a linear sum of independent components. A nonhomogenous system, which is linear apart from the presence of a function of the independent variables, is nonlinear according to a strict definition, but such systems are usually studied alongside linear systems, because they can be transformed to a linear system as long as a particular solution is known.
   a. 1-center problem
   b. George Dantzig
   c. Metric system
   d. Nonlinear system

42. The _____ fallacy is an informal fallacy. It ascribes cause where none exists. The flaw is failing to account for natural fluctuations.
   a. Depth
   b. Regression
   c. Differential
   d. Degrees of freedom

43. A _____ is the result of applying a function to a set of data.

More formally, statistical theory defines a _____ as a function of a sample where the function itself is independent of the sample's distribution: the term is used both for the function and for the value of the function on a given sample.

A _____ is distinct from an unknown statistical parameter, which is not computable from a sample.

   a. Statistic
   b. Loss function
   c. Parameter space
   d. Spatial dependence

44. _____ is a mathematical science pertaining to the collection, analysis, interpretation or explanation, and presentation of data. It also provides tools for prediction and forecasting based on data. It is applicable to a wide variety of academic disciplines, from the natural and social sciences to the humanities, government and business.
   a. Probability distribution
   b. Statistics
   c. Percentile rank
   d. Regression toward the mean

45. In mathematics, a _____ is a constant multiplicative factor of a certain object. For example, in the expression $9x^2$, the _____ of x^2 is 9.

The object can be such things as a variable, a vector, a function, etc.

   a. Fibonacci polynomials
   b. Coefficient
   c. Stability radius
   d. Multivariate division algorithm

46. In ecology, predation describes a biological interaction where a _____ (an organism that is hunting) feeds on its prey, the organism that is attacked. _____s may or may not kill their prey prior to feeding on them, but the act of predation always results in the death of the prey. The other main category of consumption is detritivory, the consumption of dead organic material (detritus.)
   a. 1-center problem
   b. 120-cell
   c. Predator
   d. Prey

Chapter 7. Algebra: Graphs, Functions, and Linear Systems

47. A _____ is is a graphical technique for presenting a data set drawn by hand or produced by a mechanical or electronic plotter. It is a graph depicting the relationship between two or more variables used, for instance, in visualising scientific data.

_____s play an important role in statistics and data analysis.

a. Dini
c. Lattice
b. C-35
d. Plot

48. A _____ is a type of display using Cartesian coordinates to display values for two variables for a set of data. The data is displayed as a collection of points, each having the value of one variable determining the position on the horizontal axis and the value of the other variable determining the position on the vertical axis. A _____ is also called a scatter chart, scatter diagram and scatter graph.

a. 2-3 heap
c. 1-center problem
b. Scatter plot
d. 120-cell

49. In statistics, given a sample $(Y_i, X_{i1}, \ldots, X_{ip})$, $i = 1, \ldots, n$ the most general form of _____ is formulated as

$$Y_i = \beta_0 + \beta_1 \phi_1(X_{i1}) + \ldots + \beta_p \phi_p(X_{ip}) + \varepsilon_i \qquad i = 1, \ldots, n$$

where $\phi_1, \ldots, \phi_p$ may be nonlinear functions.

In matrix notation this model can be written as

$$Y = X\beta + \varepsilon$$

where Y is an n × 1 column vector, X is an n × matrix, β is a × 1 vector of parameters, and ε is an n × 1 vector of errors, which are uncorrelated random variables each with expected value 0 and variance σ^2. Note that depending on the context the sample can be seen as fixed, or random.

a. Risk aversion
c. Linear model
b. Risk measure
d. Life table

50. In mathematics and computer science, _____ (also base-16, hexa or base, of 16. It uses sixteen distinct symbols, most often the symbols 0-9 to represent values zero to nine, and A, B, C, D, E, F (or a through f) to represent values ten to fifteen.

Its primary use is as a human friendly representation of binary coded values, so it is often used in digital electronics and computer engineering.

a. Radix
c. Tetradecimal
b. Factoradic
d. Hexadecimal

51. Any formula written in terms of logarithms may be said to be in _____.

In contexts including complex manifolds and algebraic geometry, a logarithmic differential form is a 1-form that, locally at least, can be written

$$\frac{df}{f}$$

for some meromorphic function f. That is, for some open covering, there are local representations of this differential form as a logarithmic derivative.

a. Laurent series
b. Holomorphic sheaf
c. Cauchy-Hadamard theorem
d. Logarithmic form

52. The function $\log_b(x)$ depends on both b and x, but the term _____ (or logarithmic function) in standard usage refers to a function of the form $\log_b(x)$ in which the base b is fixed and so the only argument is x. Thus there is one _____ for each value of the base b (which must be positive and must differ from 1.) Viewed in this way, the base-b _____ is the inverse function of the exponential function b^x.

a. 1-center problem
b. Logarithm function
c. 2-3 heap
d. 120-cell

53. Exponentiation is a mathematical operation, written a^n, involving two numbers, the base a and the _____ n. When n is a positive integer, exponentiation corresponds to repeated multiplication:

$$a^n = \underbrace{a \times \cdots \times a}_{n},$$

just as multiplication by a positive integer corresponds to repeated addition:

$$a \times n = \underbrace{a + \cdots + a}_{n}.$$

The _____ is usually shown as a superscript to the right of the base. The exponentiation a^n can be read as: a raised to the n-th power, a raised to the power [of] n or possibly a raised to the _____ [of] n, or more briefly: a to the n-th power or a to the power [of] n, or even more briefly: a to the n.

a. Exponential sum
b. Exponential tree
c. Exponentiating by squaring
d. Exponent

54. _____ generally conveys two primary meanings. The first is an imprecise sense of harmonious or aesthetically-pleasing proportionality and balance; such that it reflects beauty or perfection. The second meaning is a precise and well-defined concept of balance or 'patterned self-similarity' that can be demonstrated or proved according to the rules of a formal system: by geometry, through physics or otherwise.

a. Molecular symmetry
b. Symmetry
c. Tessellation
d. Symmetry breaking

55. In mathematics, the _____ is a conic section, the intersection of a right circular conical surface and a plane parallel to a generating straight line of that surface. Given a point and a line that lie in a plane, the locus of points in that plane that are equidistant to them is a _____.

A particular case arises when the plane is tangent to the conical surface of a circle.

a. Dandelin sphere
b. Matrix representation of conic sections
c. Directrix
d. Parabola

56. A _____, in mathematics, is a polynomial function of the form $f(x) = ax^2 + bx + c$, where $a \neq 0$. The graph of a _____ is a parabola whose major axis is parallel to the y-axis.

The expression $ax^2 + bx + c$ in the definition of a _____ is a polynomial of degree 2 or a 2nd degree polynomial, because the highest exponent of x is 2.

a. Discriminant
b. Quadratic Function
c. Laguerre polynomials
d. Multivariate division algorithm

Chapter 8. Consumer Mathematics and Financial Management

1. In mathematics, a _____ is a way of expressing a number as a fraction of 100. It is often denoted using the percent sign, '%'. For example, 45% is equal to 45 / 100, or 0.45.
   a. Percentage
   b. Lowest common denominator
   c. Subtrahend
   d. Least common multiple

2. In statistics, the _____ problem occurs when one considers a set of statistical inferences simultaneously. Errors in inference, including confidence intervals that fail to include their corresponding population parameters are more likely when one considers the family as a whole.

   The term 'comparisons' in _____ typically refers to comparisons of two groups, such as treatment versus control.

   a. Familywise error rate
   b. Closed testing procedure
   c. Cross-validation
   d. Multiple comparisons

3. The _____ Evaluation and Review Technique, commonly abbreviated PERT, is a model for project management designed to analyze and represent the tasks involved in completing a given project.

   PERT is a method to analyze the involved tasks in completing a given project, especially the time needed to complete each task, and identifying the minimum time needed to complete the total project.

   This model was invented by Booz Allen Hamilton, Inc.

   a. Huge
   b. Key server
   c. Battle of the Sexes
   d. Program

4. _____ is a fee, paid on borrowed capital. Assets lent include money, shares, consumer goods through hire purchase, major assets such as aircraft, and even entire factories in finance lease arrangements. The _____ is calculated upon the value of the assets in the same manner as upon money.
   a. Interest expense
   b. A Mathematical Theory of Communication
   c. Interest
   d. Interest sensitivity gap

5. In abstract algebra, a module S over a ring R is called _____ or irreducible if it is not the zero module 0 and if its only submodules are 0 and S. Understanding the _____ modules over a ring is usually helpful because these modules form the 'building blocks' of all other modules in a certain sense.

   Abelian groups are the same as Z-modules.

   a. Harmonic series
   b. Derivation
   c. Basis
   d. Simple

6. A calculation is a deliberate process for transforming one or more inputs into one or more results, with variable change.

   The term is used in a variety of senses, from the very definite arithmetical using an algorithm to the vague heuristics of _____ a strategy in a competition or _____ the chance of a successful relationship between two people.

Chapter 8. Consumer Mathematics and Financial Management

Multiplying 7 by 8 is a simple algorithmic calculation.

a. Mathematical maturity
b. Calculating
c. Calculation
d. Mathematics Subject Classification

7. In mathematics, _____ and undefined are used to explain whether or not expressions have meaningful, sensible, and unambiguous values. Not all branches of mathematics come to the same conclusion.

The following expressions are undefined in all contexts, but remarks in the analysis section may apply.

a. Plugging in
b. LHS
c. Toy model
d. Defined

8. _____ is the concept of adding accumulated interest back to the principal, so that interest is earned on interest from that moment on. The act of declaring interest to be principal is called compounding. A loan, for example, may have its interest compounded every month: in this case, a loan with $100 principal and 1% interest per month would have a balance of $101 at the end of the first month.

a. Net interest margin securities
b. Net interest margin
c. Retained interest
d. Compound interest

9. A _____ typically refers to a class of handheld calculators that are capable of plotting graphs, solving simultaneous equations, and performing numerous other tasks with variables. Most popular _____s are also programmable, allowing the user to create customized programs, typically for scientific/engineering and education applications. Due to their large displays intended for graphing, they can also accommodate several lines of text and calculations at a time.

a. Bump mapping
b. Genus
c. Support vector machines
d. Graphing calculator

10. A _____ is a device for performing mathematical calculations, distinguished from a computer by having a limited problem solving ability and an interface optimized for interactive calculation rather than programming. _____s can be hardware or software, and mechanical or electronic, and are often built into devices such as PDAs or mobile phones.

Modern electronic _____s are generally small, digital, and usually inexpensive.

a. 1-center problem
b. 120-cell
c. 2-3 heap
d. Calculator

11. The _____ are the set of numbers consisting of the natural numbers including 0 and their negatives. They are numbers that can be written without a fractional or decimal component, and fall within the set {... −2, −1, 0, 1, 2, ...}.

a. A chemical equation
b. A Mathematical Theory of Communication
c. A posteriori
d. Integers

12. In mathematics, a _____ is a number that can be expressed as an integral of an algebraic function over an algebraic domain. Kontsevich and Zagier define a _____ as a complex number whose real and imaginary parts are values of absolutely convergent integrals of rational functions with rational coefficients, over domains in given by polynomial inequalities with rational coefficients.

Chapter 8. Consumer Mathematics and Financial Management

a. Closeness
b. Disk
c. Period
d. Boussinesq approximation

13. In probability theory, a probability distribution is called _____ if its cumulative distribution function is _____. That is equivalent to saying that for random variables X with the distribution in question, Pr[X = a] = 0 for all real numbers a. If the distribution of X is _____ then X is called a _____ random variable.

a. Concatenated codes
b. Conull set
c. Continuous
d. Continuous phase modulation

14. The terms _____, nominal APR, and effective APR describe the interest rate for a whole year, rather than just a monthly fee/rate, as applied on a loan, mortgage, credit card, etc. Those terms have formal, legal definitions in some countries or legal jurisdictions, but in general:

- The nominal APR is the simple-interest rate.
- The effective APR is the fee+compound interest rate.

The nominal APR is calculated as: the rate, for a payment period, multiplied by the number of payment periods in a year. However, the exact legal definition of 'effective APR' can vary greatly in each jurisdiction, depending on the type of fees included, such as participation fees, loan origination fees, monthly service charges, or late fees. The effective APR has been called the 'mathematically-true' interest rate for each year. The computation for the effective APR, as the fee+compound interest rate, can also vary depending on whether the up-front fees, such as origination or participation fees, are added to the entire amount, or treated as a short-term loan due in the first payment.

a. A chemical equation
b. A posteriori
c. Annual percentage rate
d. A Mathematical Theory of Communication

15. In finance, _____ rate of profit or sometimes just return, is the ratio of money gained or lost on an investment relative to the amount of money invested. The amount of money gained or lost may be referred to as interest, profit/loss, gain/loss, or net income/loss. The money invested may be referred to as the asset, capital, principal, or the cost basis of the investment.

a. Rate of return
b. 1-center problem
c. P/E ratio
d. Return on equity

16. In mathematics and in the sciences, a _____ (plural: _____e, formulæ or _____s) is a concise way of expressing information symbolically (as in a mathematical or chemical _____), or a general relationship between quantities. One of many famous _____e is Albert Einstein's $E = mc^2$ (see special relativity)

In mathematics, a _____ is a key to solve an equation with variables. For example, the problem of determining the volume of a sphere is one that requires a significant amount of integral calculus to solve.

a. 120-cell
b. 1-center problem
c. 2-3 heap
d. Formula

Chapter 8. Consumer Mathematics and Financial Management

17. _____s are payments made by a corporation to its shareholder members. When a corporation earns a profit or surplus, that money can be put to two uses: it can either be re-invested in the business, or it can be paid to the shareholders as a _____. Many corporations retain a portion of their earnings and pay the remainder as a _____.

   a. Dividend
   b. 120-cell
   c. GNU Privacy Guard
   d. 1-center problem

18. The term _____ refers to the central sense organ complex, for those animals that have one, normally on the ventral surface of the head and can depending on the definition in the human case, include the hair, forehead, eyebrow, eyes, nose, ears, cheeks, mouth, lips, philtrum, teeth, skin, and chin. The _____ has uses of expression, appearance, and identity amongst others.It also has different senses like smelling, tasting, hearing, and seeing.

   Caricatures often exaggerate facial features to make a _____ more easily recognized in association with a pronounced portion of the _____ of the individual in question--for example, a caricature of Osama bin Laden might focus on his facial hair and nose; a caricature of George W. Bush might enlarge his ears to the size of an elephant¢s; a caricature of Jay Leno may pronounce his head and chin; and a caricature of Mick Jagger might enlarge his lips.

   a. 120-cell
   b. 2-3 heap
   c. 1-center problem
   d. Face

19. _____ is the self-government of a nation, country or some portion thereof, generally exercising sovereignty.

   The term _____ is used in contrast to subjugation, which refers to a region as a 'territory' --subject to the political and military control of an external government. The word is sometimes used in a weaker sense to contrast with hegemony, the indirect control of one nation by another, more powerful nation.

   a. A posteriori
   b. A Mathematical Theory of Communication
   c. A chemical equation
   d. Independence

20. In mathematics, an _____, or central tendency of a data set refers to a measure of the 'middle' or 'expected' value of the data set. There are many different descriptive statistics that can be chosen as a measurement of the central tendency of the data items.

   An _____ is a single value that is meant to typify a list of values.

   a. A posteriori
   b. Average
   c. A chemical equation
   d. A Mathematical Theory of Communication

21. The phrase _____ or bullet payment refers to one of two ways for repaying a loan; the other type is called amortizing payment or Amortization.

   With a balloon loan, a _____ is paid back when the loan comes to its contractual maturity, e.g. reaches the deadline set to repayment at the time the loan was granted, representing the full loan amount. Periodic interest payments are generally made throughout the life of the loan.

Chapter 8. Consumer Mathematics and Financial Management 67

  a. Balloon payment
  c. 120-cell
  b. Flow to Equity-Approach
  d. 1-center problem

22. _____ is a legal term (in some jurisdictions, notably in the USA, United Kingdom, Canada, and Australia) that encompasses land along with anything permanently affixed to the land, such as buildings, specifically property that is stationary, or fixed in location. _____ law is the body of regulations and legal codes which pertain to such matters under a particular jurisdiction. _____ is often considered synonymous with real property (also sometimes called realty), in contrast with personal property (also sometimes called chattel or personalty under chattel law or personal property law.)
  a. Home equity
  c. Real estate
  b. 120-cell
  d. 1-center problem

23. In economics, business, retail, and accounting, a _____ is the value of money that has been used up to produce something, and hence is not available for use anymore. In business, the _____ may be one of acquisition, in which case the amount of money expended to acquire it is counted as _____. In this case, money is the input that is gone in order to acquire the thing.
  a. 1-center problem
  c. 120-cell
  b. 2-3 heap
  d. Cost

24. A _____ is the transfer of an interest in property (or in law the equivalent - a charge) to a lender as a security for a debt - usually a loan of money. While a _____ in itself is not a debt, it is lender's security for a debt. It is a transfer of an interest in land (or the equivalent), from the owner to the _____ lender, on the condition that this interest will be returned to the owner of the real estate when the terms of the _____ have been satisfied or performed.
  a. 1-center problem
  c. 120-cell
  b. 2-3 heap
  d. Mortgage

25. _____ is a general term for any type of information processing. This includes phenomena ranging from human thinking to calculations with a more narrow meaning. _____ is a process following a well-defined model that is understood and can be expressed in an algorithm, protocol, network topology, etc.
  a. Computation
  c. 120-cell
  b. 2-3 heap
  d. 1-center problem

26. _____ or amortisation is the process of decreasing an amount over a period of time. The word comes from Middle English amortisen to kill, alienate in mortmain, from Anglo-French amorteser, alteration of amortir, from Vulgar Latin admortire to kill, from Latin ad- + mort-, mors death. Particular instances of the term include:

- _____, the allocation of a lump sum amount to different time periods, particularly for loans and other forms of finance, including related interest or other finance charges.
    - _____ schedule, a table detailing each periodic payment on a loan, as generated by an _____ calculator.
    - Negative _____, an _____ schedule where the loan amount actually increases through not paying the full interest
- Amortized analysis, analyzing the execution cost of algorithms over a sequence of operations.
- _____ of capital expenditures of certain assets under accounting rules, particularly intangible assets, in a manner analogous to depreciation.
- _____

Chapter 8. Consumer Mathematics and Financial Management

_____ is also used in the context of zoning regulations and describes the time in which a property owner has to relocate when the property's use constitutes a preexisting nonconforming use under zoning regulations.

- Depreciation

a. ISAAC
c. Identity
b. Origin
d. Amortization

27. A _____ is a theoretical region of space in which the gravitational field is so powerful that nothing, not even electromagnetic radiation, can escape its pull after having fallen past its event horizon. The term derives from the fact that the absorption of visible light renders the hole's interior invisible, and indistinguishable from the black space around it.

Despite its interior being invisible, a _____ may reveal its presence through an interaction with matter that lies in orbit outside its event horizon.

a. Skew
c. Genus
b. Common operator notation
d. Black hole

28. An _____ is a table detailing each periodic payment on a amortizing loan, as generated by an amortization calculator.

While a portion of every payment is applied towards both the interest and the principal balance of the loan, the exact amount applied to principal each time varies. An _____ reveals the specific monetary amount put towards interest, as well as the specific put towards the Principal balance, with each payment.

a. A Mathematical Theory of Communication
c. A chemical equation
b. Accounts receivable
d. Amortization schedule

29. '_____ in many usages, including economic ones, may express ethical acceptance of some possible social stat against which other possible social states are measured. By contrast, the usage of justice in economics is as a subcategory of welfare economics with models frequently representing the ethical-social requirements of a given theory. That theory may or may not elicit acceptance.
a. Completely randomized designs
c. Complex Mexican hat wavelet
b. Just'
d. Contrapositive

30. In mathematics, the _____ of a number n is the number that, when added to n, yields zero. The _____ of n is denoted −n. For example, 7 is −7, because 7 + (−7) = 0, and the _____ of −0.3 is 0.3, because −0.3 + 0.3 = 0.
a. Associativity
c. Arity
b. Algebraic structure
d. Additive inverse

Chapter 9. Measurement

1. The framework of quantum mechanics requires a careful definition of _____, and a thorough discussion of its practical and philosophical implications.

_____ is viewed in different ways in the many interpretations of quantum mechanics; however, despite the considerable philosophical differences, they almost universally agree on the practical question of what results from a routine quantum-physics laboratory _____. To describe this, a simple framework to use is the Copenhagen interpretation, and it will be implicitly used in this section; the utility of this approach has been verified countless times, and all other interpretations are necessarily constructed so as to give the same quantitative predictions as this in almost every case.

   a. Measurement
   c. 1-center problem
   b. Dynamic range
   d. Fundamental units

2. _____ is a conceptual tool often applied in physics, chemistry, engineering, mathematics and statistics to understand physical situations involving a mix of different kinds of physical quantities. It is routinely used by physical scientists and engineers to check the plausibility of derived equations and computations. It is also used to form reasonable hypotheses about complex physical situations that can be tested by experiment or by more developed theories of the phenomena.
   a. 1-center problem
   c. 2-3 heap
   b. 120-cell
   d. Dimensional analysis

3. A _____ is a mathematical model of a system based on the use of a linear operator. _____s typically exhibit features and properties that are much simpler than the general, nonlinear case. As a mathematical abstraction or idealization, _____s find important applications in automatic control theory, signal processing, and telecommunications.
   a. Hybrid system
   c. Predispositioning Theory
   b. Percolation
   d. Linear system

4. _____ is a quantity expressing the two-dimensional size of a defined part of a surface, typically a region bounded by a closed curve. The term surface _____ refers to the total _____ of the exposed surface of a 3-dimensional solid, such as the sum of the _____s of the exposed sides of a polyhedron. _____ is an important invariant in the differential geometry of surfaces.
   a. A chemical equation
   c. A posteriori
   b. A Mathematical Theory of Communication
   d. Area

5. In mathematics, _____ and undefined are used to explain whether or not expressions have meaningful, sensible, and unambiguous values. Not all branches of mathematics come to the same conclusion.

The following expressions are undefined in all contexts, but remarks in the analysis section may apply.

   a. Plugging in
   c. Toy model
   b. LHS
   d. Defined

6. In mathematics the concept of a _____ generalizes notions such as 'length', 'area', and 'volume'. Informally, given some base set, a '_____' is any consistent assignment of 'sizes' to the subsets of the base set. Depending on the application, the 'size' of a subset may be interpreted as its physical size, the amount of something that lies within the subset, or the probability that some random process will yield a result within the subset.

a. Lattice	b. Measure
c. Cusp	d. Congruent

7. The _____ is a decimalised system of measurement. It exists in several variations, with different choices of base units, though the choice of base units does not affect its day-to-day use. Over the last two centuries, different variants have been considered the _____.

a. Nonlinear system	b. George Dantzig
c. Metric system	d. 1-center problem

8. A _____ is a type of affix attached to a stem which modifies the meaning of that stem.

The word '_____' is itself made up of the stem fix, and the _____ pre-, both of which are derived from Latin roots.

- English _____ es
- _____ es and suffixes in Hebrew

a. 120-cell	b. 1-center problem
c. 2-3 heap	d. Prefix

9. The _____ of a material is defined as its mass per unit volume:

$$\rho = \frac{m}{V}$$

Different materials usually have different densities, so _____ is an important concept regarding buoyancy, metal purity and packaging.

In some cases _____ is expressed as the dimensionless quantities specific gravity or relative _____, in which case it is expressed in multiples of the _____ of some other standard material, usually water or air.

In a well-known story, Archimedes was given the task of determining whether King Hiero's goldsmith was embezzling gold during the manufacture of a wreath dedicated to the gods and replacing it with another, cheaper alloy.

a. 120-cell	b. 1-center problem
c. 2-3 heap	d. Density

10. _____ is a part of mathematics concerned with questions of size, shape, and relative position of figures and with properties of space. _____ is one of the oldest sciences. Initially a body of practical knowledge concerning lengths, areas, and volumes, in the third century BC _____ was put into an axiomatic form by Euclid, whose treatment--Euclidean _____--set a standard for many centuries to follow.

Chapter 9. Measurement 71

   a. 1-center problem
   c. Geometry
   b. 120-cell
   d. 2-3 heap

11. In geometry and trigonometry, an _____ is the figure formed by two rays sharing a common endpoint, called the vertex of the _____. The magnitude of the _____ is the 'amount of rotation' that separates the two rays, and can be measured by considering the length of circular arc swept out when one ray is rotated about the vertex to coincide with the other. Where there is no possibility of confusion, the term '_____' is used interchangeably for both the geometric configuration itself and for its angular magnitude.
   a. A chemical equation
   c. A posteriori
   b. A Mathematical Theory of Communication
   d. Angle

12. In mathematics, the _____ or Pythagoras' theorem is a relation in Euclidean geometry among the three sides of a right triangle. The theorem is named after the Greek mathematician Pythagoras, who by tradition is credited with its discovery and proof, although it is often argued that knowledge of the theory predates him.. The theorem is as follows:

In any right triangle, the area of the square whose side is the hypotenuse is equal to the sum of the areas of the squares whose sides are the two legs.

   a. 2-3 heap
   c. 1-center problem
   b. Pythagorean Theorem
   d. 120-cell

13. In mathematics, a _____ is a statement that can be proved on the basis of explicitly stated or previously agreed assumptions.
   a. Logical value
   c. Disjunction introduction
   b. Boolean function
   d. Theorem

14. The _____ of any solid, plasma, vacuum or theoretical object is how much three-dimensional space it occupies, often quantified numerically. One-dimensional figures and two-dimensional shapes are assigned zero _____ in the three-dimensional space. _____ is presented as ml or cm^3.

_____s of straight-edged and circular shapes are calculated using arithmetic formulae.

   a. Cauchy momentum equation
   c. Volume
   b. Thermodynamic limit
   d. Stress-energy tensor

15. In the physical sciences, _____ is a measurement of the gravitational force acting on an object. Near the surface of the Earth, the acceleration due to gravity is approximately constant; this means that an object's _____ is roughly proportional to its mass.

In commerce and in many other applications, _____ means the same as mass as that term is used in physics.

   a. 2-3 heap
   c. 120-cell
   b. 1-center problem
   d. Weight

Chapter 9. Measurement

16. Celsius is a temperature scale that is named after the Swedish astronomer Anders Celsius, who developed a similar temperature scale two years before his death. The degree Celsius can refer to a specific temperature on the _____ as well as serve as a unit increment to indicate a temperature interval.

From 1744 until 1954, 0 °C on the _____ was defined as the freezing point of water and 100 °C was defined as the boiling point of water under a pressure of one standard atmosphere; this close equivalency is taught in schools today.

- a. Celsius scale
- b. 2-3 heap
- c. 1-center problem
- d. 120-cell

17. _____ is a temperature scale that is named after the German physicist Daniel Gabriel _____, who proposed it in 1724.

In this scale, the freezing point of water is 32 degrees _____ and the boiling point 212 °F, placing the boiling and freezing points of water exactly 180 degrees apart. A degree on the _____ scale is 1/180th part of the interval between the ice point and the boiling point.

- a. 120-cell
- b. 2-3 heap
- c. 1-center problem
- d. Fahrenheit

Chapter 10. Geometry

1. _____ is a part of mathematics concerned with questions of size, shape, and relative position of figures and with properties of space. _____ is one of the oldest sciences. Initially a body of practical knowledge concerning lengths, areas, and volumes, in the third century BC _____ was put into an axiomatic form by Euclid, whose treatment--Euclidean _____--set a standard for many centuries to follow.
    a. 120-cell
    b. 2-3 heap
    c. Geometry
    d. 1-center problem

2. _____ is a numeral system in which each position is related to the next by a constant multiplier, a common ratio, called the base or radix of that numeral system.
    a. Place value
    b. Cyrillic numerals
    c. Negative base
    d. NegaFibonacci coding

3. In mathematics, _____ and undefined are used to explain whether or not expressions have meaningful, sensible, and unambiguous values. Not all branches of mathematics come to the same conclusion.

    The following expressions are undefined in all contexts, but remarks in the analysis section may apply.

    a. Toy model
    b. Defined
    c. LHS
    d. Plugging in

4. In mathematics, the _____ is an approach to finding a particular solution to certain inhomogeneous ordinary differential equations and recurrence relations. It is closely related to the annihilator method, but instead of using a particular kind of differential operator in order to find the best possible form of the particular solution, a 'guess' is made as to the appropriate form, which is then tested by differentiating the resulting equation. In this sense, the _____ is less formal but more intuitive than the annihilator method.
    a. Differential algebraic equations
    b. Phase line
    c. Linear differential equation
    d. Method of undetermined coefficients

5. In mathematics, a _____ is, informally, an infinitely vast and infinitely thin sheet. _____s may be thought of as objects in some higher dimensional space, or they may be considered without any outside space, as in the setting of Euclidean geometry
    a. Bandwidth
    b. Plane
    c. Blocking
    d. Group

6. In mathematics, _____ are two-dimensional manifolds or surfaces that are perfectly flat.
    a. 120-cell
    b. 2-3 heap
    c. 1-center problem
    d. Planes

7. In geometry and trigonometry, an _____ is the figure formed by two rays sharing a common endpoint, called the vertex of the _____. The magnitude of the _____ is the 'amount of rotation' that separates the two rays, and can be measured by considering the length of circular arc swept out when one ray is rotated about the vertex to coincide with the other. Where there is no possibility of confusion, the term '_____' is used interchangeably for both the geometric configuration itself and for its angular magnitude.
    a. A Mathematical Theory of Communication
    b. Angle
    c. A posteriori
    d. A chemical equation

8. Initial objects are also called _____, and terminal objects are also called final.

Chapter 10. Geometry

a. Terminal object
b. Colimit
c. Coterminal
d. Direct limit

9. In geometry, a _____ is a part of a line that is bounded by two distinct end points, and contains every point on the line between its end points. Examples of _____s include the sides of a triangle or square. More generally, when the end points are both vertices of a polygon, the _____ is either an edge if they are adjacent vertices, or otherwise a diagonal.
    a. Golden angle
    b. Cuboid
    c. Transversal line
    d. Line segment

10. In mathematics the concept of a _____ generalizes notions such as 'length', 'area', and 'volume'. Informally, given some base set, a '_____' is any consistent assignment of 'sizes' to the subsets of the base set. Depending on the application, the 'size' of a subset may be interpreted as its physical size, the amount of something that lies within the subset, or the probability that some random process will yield a result within the subset.
    a. Congruent
    b. Lattice
    c. Cusp
    d. Measure

11. In geometry, a _____ is a special kind of point, usually a corner of a polygon, polyhedron, or higher dimensional polytope. In the geometry of curves a _____ is a point of where the first derivative of curvature is zero. In graph theory, a _____ is the fundamental unit out of which graphs are formed
    a. Duality
    b. Crib
    c. Dini
    d. Vertex

12. An angle smaller than a right angle is called an _____ (less than 90 degrees).
    a. Integral geometry
    b. Euclidean geometry
    c. Ultraparallel theorem
    d. Acute angle

13. In discrete mathematics and predominantly in set theory, a _____ is a concept used in comparisons of sets to refer to the unique values of one set in relation to another. The terms 'absolute' and 'relative' _____ refer to more specific applications of the concept, with universal _____s referring to elements unique to the universal set and the latter referring to the unique elements of one set in relation to another. In this image, the universal set is represented by the border of the image, and the set A as a disc.
    a. Kernel
    b. Huge
    c. Derivative algebra
    d. Complement

14. A pair of angles are complementary if the sum of their measures add up to 90 degrees.

If the two _____ are adjacent (i.e. have a common vertex and share a side, but do not have any interior points in common) their non-shared sides form a right angle.

In Euclidean geometry, the two acute angles in a right triangle are complementary, because there are 180>° in a triangle and 90>° have been accounted for by the right angle.

a. Hypotenuse
b. Quincunx
c. Conway polyhedron notation
d. Complementary angles

15. In geometry and trigonometry, a _____ is defined as an angle between two straight intersecting lines of ninety degrees, or one-quarter of a circle.
   a. Trigonometry
   b. Trigonometric functions
   c. Sine integral
   d. Right angle

16. An angle equal to two right angles is called a _____ (equal to 180 degrees).
   a. Loomis-Whitney inequality
   b. Householder transformation
   c. Straight angle
   d. Theorem

17. A pair of angles is _____ if their measurements add up to 180 degrees. If the two _____ angles are adjacent their non-shared sides form a straight line. The supplement of 135 would be 45.
   a. FISH
   b. Dense
   c. Cylinder
   d. Supplementary

18. A pair of angles are said to be _____ if they share the same vertex and are bounded by the same pair of lines but are opposite to each other. They are also congruent.
   a. Reflection symmetry
   b. Hinge theorem
   c. Line segment
   d. Vertical angles

19. A _____ of a curve is the envelope of a family of congruent circles centered on the curve. It generalises the concept of _____ lines.

It is sometimes called the offset curve but the term 'offset' often refers also to translation.

   a. Bifolium
   b. Cycloid
   c. Cissoid
   d. Parallel

20. The existence and properties of _____ are the basis of Euclid's parallel postulate. _____ are two lines on the same plane that do not intersect even assuming that lines extend to infinity in either direction.
   a. Vertical translation
   b. Parallel lines
   c. Square wheel
   d. Spidron

21. _____ are formed when a given transversal line crosses two coplanar lines. The _____ are not necessarily congruent. In the event that the _____ are congruent, these angles can be used to determine the degrees of the other angles of the parallel lines.
   a. Brocard circle
   b. Prismatic pentagonal tiling
   c. Corresponding angles
   d. Conformal connection

22. In combinatorial mathematics, given a collection C of sets, a _____ is a set containing exactly one element from each member of the collection: it is a section of the quotient map induced by the collection. If the original sets are not disjoint, there are several different definitions. One variation is that there is a bijection f from the _____ to C such that x is an element of f
   a. Heawood number
   b. Combinatorial design
   c. Combinadic
   d. Transversal

23. In general topology and related areas of mathematics, the _____ (inductive topology or strong topology) on a set X, with respect to a family of functions into X, is the finest topology on X which makes those functions continuous.

Given a set X and a family of topological spaces Y_i with functions

$$f_i : Y_i \to X$$

the _____ τ on X is the finest topology such that each

$$f_i : Y_i \to (X, \tau)$$

is continuous.

Explicitly, the _____ may be described as follows: a subset U of X is open if and only if $f_i^{-1}(U)$ is open in Y_i for each i ∈ I.

a. Wallman compactification
c. Gluing axiom
b. Cylinder set
d. Final topology

24. An _____ is an angle formed by one side of a simple polygon and a line extended from that side.
a. Angular diameter
c. Interior angle
b. Orthogon
d. Exterior Angle

25. In geometry, an _____ is an angle formed by two sides of a simple polygon that share an endpoint, namely, the angle on the inner side of the polygon. A simple polygon has exactly one internal angle per vertex.

If every internal angle of a polygon is at most 180 degrees, the polygon is called convex.

a. Exterior angle
c. Angle bisector
b. Angle chasing
d. Interior Angle

26. _____ or set diagrams are diagrams that show all hypothetically possible logical relations between a finite collection of sets. _____ were invented around 1880 by John Venn. They are used in many fields, including set theory, probability, logic, statistics, and computer science.
a. Venn diagrams
c. 1-center problem
b. 2-3 heap
d. 120-cell

27. In mathematics, _____ is a property that a binary operation can have. It means that, within an expression containing two or more of the same associative operators in a row, the order that the operations are performed does not matter as long as the sequence of the operands is not changed. That is, rearranging the parentheses in such an expression will not change its value.
a. Unital
c. Algebraically closed
b. Idempotence
d. Associativity

Chapter 10. Geometry

28. A _____ is a 2D geometric symbolic representation of information according to some visualization technique. Sometimes, the technique uses a 3D visualization which is then projected onto the 2D surface. The word graph is sometimes used as a synonym for _____.
   a. 1-center problem
   b. Diagram
   c. 2-3 heap
   d. 120-cell

29. _____ consists of mental processes of discernment, analysis and evaluation. It includes possible processes of reflecting upon a tangible or intangible item in order to form a solid judgment that reconciles scientific evidence with common sense. In contemporary usage 'critical' has a certain negative connotation that does not apply in the present case.
   a. Counterpart theory
   b. Parametric operator
   c. Finite model property
   d. Critical thinking

30. In mathematics, an _____ or member of a set is any one of the distinct objects that make up that set.

Writing A = {1,2,3,4}, means that the _____s of the set A are the numbers 1, 2, 3 and 4. Groups of _____s of A, for example {1,2}, are subsets of A.

   a. Order
   b. Universal code
   c. Element
   d. Ideal

31. In mathematics, a _____ is a statement that can be proved on the basis of explicitly stated or previously agreed assumptions.
   a. Logical value
   b. Boolean function
   c. Disjunction introduction
   d. Theorem

32. A _____ is one of the basic shapes of geometry: a polygon with three corners or vertices and three sides or edges which are line segments. A _____ with vertices A, B, and C is denoted ABC.

In Euclidean geometry any three non-collinear points determine a unique _____ and a unique plane.

   a. Triangle
   b. 1-center problem
   c. Kepler triangle
   d. Fuhrmann circle

33. In geometry, an _____ is a triangle in which all three sides have equal lengths. In traditional or Euclidean geometry, _____s are also equiangular; that is, all three internal angles are also equal to each other and are each 60°. They are regular polygons, and can therefore also be referred to as regular triangles.
   a. A chemical equation
   b. Isotomic conjugate
   c. A Mathematical Theory of Communication
   d. Equilateral triangle

34. In mathematics, the _____ or Pythagoras' theorem is a relation in Euclidean geometry among the three sides of a right triangle. The theorem is named after the Greek mathematician Pythagoras, who by tradition is credited with its discovery and proof, although it is often argued that knowledge of the theory predates him.. The theorem is as follows:

In any right triangle, the area of the square whose side is the hypotenuse is equal to the sum of the areas of the squares whose sides are the two legs.

a. 2-3 heap
c. Pythagorean Theorem
b. 1-center problem
d. 120-cell

35. In mathematics, the _____ of a ring R, often denoted cha, is defined to be the smallest number of times one must add the ring's multiplicative identity element to itself to get the additive identity element; the ring is said to have _____ zero if this repeated sum never reaches the additive identity. That is, cha is the smallest positive number n such that

$$\underbrace{1 + \cdots + 1}_{n \text{ summands}} = 0$$

if such a number n exists, and 0 otherwise. The _____ may also be taken to be the exponent of the ring's additive group, that is, the smallest positive n such that

$$\underbrace{a + \cdots + a}_{n \text{ summands}} = 0$$

for every element a of the ring.

a. Class
c. Coherent
b. Disk
d. Characteristic

36. In geometry, a number of tests for congruence and similarity involve comparing _____. In such tests, each side in one figure is paired with a side in the second figure, taking care to preserve the order of adjacency - in other words, if side A in figure #1 is adjacent to sides B and C, and its pair in figure #2 is side X which is adjacent to sides Y and Z, then B and C must be paired with Y and Z in either order. The pairs of sides are then known as _____.

a. Non-Euclidean geometry
c. The Geometry Center
b. Prismatic surface
d. Corresponding sides

37. In linear algebra, two n-by-n matrices A and B over the field K are called _____ if there exists an invertible n-by-n matrix P over K such that

$$P^{-1}AP = B.$$

One of the meanings of the term similarity transformation is such a transformation of a matrix A into a matrix B.

Similarity is an equivalence relation on the space of square matrices.

_____ matrices share many properties:

- rank
- determinant
- trace
- eigenvalues
- characteristic polynomial
- minimal polynomial
- elementary divisors

There are two reasons for these facts:

- two _____ matrices can be thought of as describing the same linear map, but with respect to different bases
- the map $X \mapsto P^{-1}XP$ is an automorphism of the associative algebra of all n-by-n matrices, as the one-object case of the above category of all matrices.

Because of this, for a given matrix A, one is interested in finding a simple 'normal form' B which is _____ to A -- the study of A then reduces to the study of the simpler matrix B.

a. Dense
c. Coherence
b. Blinding
d. Similar

38. A _____ is the longest side of a right triangle, the side opposite of the right angle. The length of the _____ of a right triangle can be found using the Pythagorean theorem, which states that the square of the length of the _____ equals the sum of the squares of the lengths of the two other sides.

For example, if one of the other sides has a length of 3 meters and the other has a length of 4 m.

a. Concyclic points
c. Golden angle
b. Hypotenuse
d. Reflection symmetry

39. In a right triangle, the cathetusoriginally from the Greek word Κἀθετος, plural catheti

- 1 Generally
- 2 References
- 3 See also
- 4 External links

In a wider sense, a _____ is any line falling perpendicularly on another line or a surface. Such a line is more commonly known as a surface normal.

a. Face diagonal
b. Line segment
c. Central angle
d. Cathetus

40. The _____ is the length of the line that bounds an area In the special case where the area is circular, the _____ is known as the circumference.
   a. Reflection symmetry
   b. Multilateration
   c. Concyclic
   d. Perimeter

41. In geometry a _____ is traditionally a plane figure that is bounded by a closed path or circuit, composed of a finite sequence of straight line segments. These segments are called its edges or sides, and the points where two edges meet are the _____'s vertices or corners. The interior of the _____ is sometimes called its body.
   a. Regular polygon
   b. Polygonal curve
   c. Parallelogon
   d. Polygon

42. In geometry, a _____ is a polygon with four sides or edges and four vertices or corners. Sometimes, the term quadrangle is used, for etymological symmetry with triangle, and sometimes tetragon for consistency with pentagon, hexagon and so on. The interior angles of a _____ add up to 360 degrees of arc.
   a. 1-center problem
   b. 120-cell
   c. 2-3 heap
   d. Quadrilateral

43. A _____ is a polygon which is equiangular and equilateral. _____s may be convex or star.

These properties apply to both convex and star _____s.

   a. Regular decagon
   b. Constructible polygon
   c. Regular polygon
   d. Star-shaped polygon

44. _____ are used in computer graphics to compose images that are three-dimensional in appearance. Usually triangular, _____ arise when an object's surface is modeled, vertices are selected, and the object is rendered in a wire frame model. This is quicker to display than a shaded model; thus the _____ are a stage in computer animation.
   a. Visibility polygon
   b. Triskaidecagon
   c. Heptadecagon
   d. Polygons

45. In geometry, a _____ is a polygon with six edges and six vertices. A regular _____ has Schläfli symbol {6}.

The internal angles of a regular _____ are all 120° and the _____ has 720 degrees.

   a. Polygonal curve
   b. Polygonal chain
   c. Decagon
   d. Hexagon

46. In geometry, a _____ , or rhomb is an equilateral parallelogram. In other words, it is a four-sided polygon in which every side has the same length.

The _____ is often casually called a diamond, after the diamonds suit in playing cards, or a lozenge, because those shapes are rhombi, although rhombi are not necessarily diamonds or lozenges.

Chapter 10. Geometry

a. 120-cell
c. 1-center problem
b. 2-3 heap
d. Rhombus

47. A _____ or a trapezium is a quadrilateral that has at least one pair of parallel lines for sides.

Some authors define it as a quadrilateral having exactly one pair of parallel sides, so as to exclude parallelograms, which otherwise would be regarded as a special type of _____, but most mathematicians use the inclusive definition.

In North America, the term trapezium is used to refer to a quadrilateral with no parallel sides.

a. Lozenge
c. Trapezium
b. Rhomboid
d. Trapezoid

48. A _____ or tiling of the plane is a collection of plane figures that fills the plane with no overlaps and no gaps. One may also speak of _____s of the parts of the plane or of other surfaces. Generalizations to higher dimensions are also possible.

a. Directional symmetry
c. Symmetry breaking
b. Molecular symmetry
d. Tessellation

49. _____ was the Allied codename for any of several German teleprinter stream ciphers used during World War II. Enciphered teleprinter traffic was used between German High Command and Army Group commanders in the field, so its intelligence value was of the highest strategic value to the Allies. This traffic normally passed over landlines, but as German forces extended their reach out of western Europe, they had to resort to wireless transmission.

a. Divide and conquer
c. Function
b. Colossus
d. Fish

50. _____ generally conveys two primary meanings. The first is an imprecise sense of harmonious or aesthetically-pleasing proportionality and balance; such that it reflects beauty or perfection. The second meaning is a precise and well-defined concept of balance or 'patterned self-similarity' that can be demonstrated or proved according to the rules of a formal system: by geometry, through physics or otherwise.

a. Symmetry
c. Tessellation
b. Molecular symmetry
d. Symmetry breaking

51. _____ is a quantity expressing the two-dimensional size of a defined part of a surface, typically a region bounded by a closed curve. The term surface _____ refers to the total _____ of the exposed surface of a 3-dimensional solid, such as the sum of the _____s of the exposed sides of a polyhedron. _____ is an important invariant in the differential geometry of surfaces.

a. A posteriori
c. A chemical equation
b. A Mathematical Theory of Communication
d. Area

52. In mathematics and in the sciences, a _____ (plural: _____e, formulæ or _____s) is a concise way of expressing information symbolically (as in a mathematical or chemical _____), or a general relationship between quantities. One of many famous _____e is Albert Einstein's $E = mc^2$ (see special relativity

In mathematics, a _____ is a key to solve an equation with variables. For example, the problem of determining the volume of a sphere is one that requires a significant amount of integral calculus to solve.

a. 2-3 heap
b. 120-cell
c. 1-center problem
d. Formula

53. In geometry, a _____ is defined as a quadrilateral where all four of its angles are right angles.
a. Point group in two dimensions
b. Rectangle
c. Polytope
d. Cantor-Dedekind axiom

54. In mathematics and computer science, _____ (also base-16, hexa or base, of 16. It uses sixteen distinct symbols, most often the symbols 0-9 to represent values zero to nine, and A, B, C, D, E, F (or a through f) to represent values ten to fifteen.

Its primary use is as a human friendly representation of binary coded values, so it is often used in digital electronics and computer engineering.

a. Factoradic
b. Radix
c. Tetradecimal
d. Hexadecimal

55. _____ is the measurement of vertical distance, but has two meanings in common use. It can either indicate how 'tall' something is, or how 'high up' it is. For example one could say 'That is a tall building', or 'That airplane is high up in the sky'.
a. 1-center problem
b. Height
c. 2-3 heap
d. 120-cell

56. Any formula written in terms of logarithms may be said to be in _____.

In contexts including complex manifolds and algebraic geometry, a logarithmic differential form is a 1-form that, locally at least, can be written

$$\frac{df}{f}$$

for some meromorphic function f. That is, for some open covering, there are local representations of this differential form as a logarithmic derivative.

a. Laurent series
b. Holomorphic sheaf
c. Cauchy-Hadamard theorem
d. Logarithmic form

57. In geometry, a _____ is a quadrilateral with two sets of parallel sides. The opposite sides of a _____ are of equal length, and the opposite angles of a _____ are congruent. The three-dimensional counterpart of a _____ is a parallelepiped.

Chapter 10. Geometry

   a. 120-cell
   c. 1-center problem
   b. 2-3 heap
   d. Parallelogram

58. The term _____ or centre is used in various contexts in abstract algebra to denote the set of all those elements that commute with all other elements. More specifically:

- The _____ of a group G consists of all those elements x in G such that xg = gx for all g in G. This is a normal subgroup of G.
- The _____ of a ring R is the subset of R consisting of all those elements x of R such that xr = rx for all r in R. The _____ is a commutative subring of R, so R is an algebra over its _____.
- The _____ of an algebra A consists of all those elements x of A such that xa = ax for all a in A. See also: central simple algebra.
- The _____ of a Lie algebra L consists of all those elements x in L such that [x,a] = 0 for all a in L. This is an ideal of the Lie algebra L.
- The _____ of a monoidal category C consists of pairs *a natural isomorphism satisfying certain axioms*.

   a. Brute Force
   c. Block size
   b. Disk
   d. Center

59. A _____ is a simple shape of Euclidean geometry consisting of those points in a plane which are at a constant distance, called the radius, from a fixed point, called the center. A _____ with center A is sometimes denoted by the symbol A.

A chord of a _____ is a line segment whose two endpoints lie on the _____.

   a. Circular segment
   c. Circumcircle
   b. Circle
   d. Malfatti circles

60. In classical geometry, a _____ of a circle or sphere is any line segment from its center to its boundary. By extension, the _____ of a circle or sphere is the length of any such segment. The _____ is half the diameter. In science and engineering the term _____ of curvature is commonly used as a synonym for _____.
   a. Birational geometry
   c. Duoprism
   b. Non-Euclidean geometry
   d. Radius

61. The _____ is the distance around a closed curve. _____ is a kind of perimeter.

The _____ of a circle is the length around it.

   a. Circumference
   c. Compactness measure of a shape
   b. Brascamp-Lieb inequality
   d. Flatness

Chapter 10. Geometry

62. A _____ typically refers to a class of handheld calculators that are capable of plotting graphs, solving simultaneous equations, and performing numerous other tasks with variables. Most popular _____s are also programmable, allowing the user to create customized programs, typically for scientific/engineering and education applications. Due to their large displays intended for graphing, they can also accommodate several lines of text and calculations at a time.

    a. Graphing calculator
    b. Genus
    c. Support vector machines
    d. Bump mapping

63. A _____ is a device for performing mathematical calculations, distinguished from a computer by having a limited problem solving ability and an interface optimized for interactive calculation rather than programming. _____s can be hardware or software, and mechanical or electronic, and are often built into devices such as PDAs or mobile phones.

Modern electronic _____s are generally small, digital, and usually inexpensive.

    a. 120-cell
    b. 2-3 heap
    c. 1-center problem
    d. Calculator

64. The _____ are the set of numbers consisting of the natural numbers including 0 and their negatives. They are numbers that can be written without a fractional or decimal component, and fall within the set {... −2, −1, 0, 1, 2, ...}.

    a. A chemical equation
    b. A Mathematical Theory of Communication
    c. A posteriori
    d. Integers

65. The _____ of any solid, plasma, vacuum or theoretical object is how much three-dimensional space it occupies, often quantified numerically. One-dimensional figures and two-dimensional shapes are assigned zero _____ in the three-dimensional space. _____ is presented as ml or cm^3.

_____s of straight-edged and circular shapes are calculated using arithmetic formulae.

    a. Stress-energy tensor
    b. Cauchy momentum equation
    c. Thermodynamic limit
    d. Volume

66. The _____ of an object located in some space refers to the part of space occupied by the object as determined by its external boundary -- abstracting from other aspects the object may have such as its colour, content as well as from the object's position and orientation in space, and its size.

According to famous mathematician and statistician David George Kendall, _____ may be defined as

Simple two-dimensional _____s can be described by basic geometry such as points, line, curves, plane, and so on. _____s that occur in the physical world are often quite complex; they may be arbitrarily curved as studied by differential geometry as for plants or coastlines.)

    a. Parallel lines
    b. Spidron
    c. Confocal
    d. Shape

Chapter 10. Geometry

67. The term _____ refers to the central sense organ complex, for those animals that have one, normally on the ventral surface of the head and can depending on the definition in the human case, include the hair, forehead, eyebrow, eyes, nose, ears, cheeks, mouth, lips, philtrum, teeth, skin, and chin. The _____ has uses of expression, appearance, and identity amongst others. It also has different senses like smelling, tasting, hearing, and seeing.

Caricatures often exaggerate facial features to make a _____ more easily recognized in association with a pronounced portion of the _____ of the individual in question--for example, a caricature of Osama bin Laden might focus on his facial hair and nose; a caricature of George W. Bush might enlarge his ears to the size of an elephant¢s; a caricature of Jay Leno may pronounce his head and chin; and a caricature of Mick Jagger might enlarge his lips.

- a. 120-cell
- c. 2-3 heap
- b. 1-center problem
- d. Face

68. A _____ is often defined as a geometric object with flat faces and straight edges .

This definition of a _____ is not very precise, and to a modern mathematician is quite unsatisfactory. Grünbaum observed that:

The Original Sin in the theory of polyhedra goes back to Euclid, and through Kepler, Poinsot, Cauchy and many others ...

- a. 120-cell
- c. 2-3 heap
- b. 1-center problem
- d. Polyhedron

69. A _____ is a building where the upper surfaces are triangular and converge on one point. The base of _____s are usually quadrilateral or trilateral, meaning that a _____ usually has four or five faces. A _____'s design, with the majority of the weight closer to the ground, means that less material higher up on the _____ will be pushing down from above.

- a. 120-cell
- c. Pyramid
- b. 1-center problem
- d. 2-3 heap

70. A _____ is a three-dimensional geometric shape that tapers smoothly from a flat, round base to a point called the apex or vertex. More precisely, it is the solid figure bounded by a plane base and the surface formed by the locus of all straight line segments joining the apex to the perimeter of the base. The term '_____' sometimes refers just to the surface of this solid figure, or just to the lateral surface.

- a. Blocking
- c. Characteristic
- b. Gravity waves
- d. Cone

71. In mathematics, a _____ is a quadric surface, with the following equation in Cartesian coordinates: $(x/_a)^2 + (y/_b)^2 = 1$.

- a. Derivative algebra
- c. Free
- b. Discontinuity
- d. Cylinder

72. _____ is a three-dimensional geometric shape formed by straight lines through a fixed point vertex to the points of a fixed curve directrix.

a. 1-center problem
c. 120-cell
b. Right circular cone
d. 2-3 heap

73. In common usage, a cylinder is taken to mean a finite section of a _____ with its ends closed to form two circular surfaces, as in the figure (right.) If the cylinder has a radius r and length (height) h, then its volume is given by

$$V = \pi r^2 h$$

and its surface area is:

- the area of the top (πr^2) +
- the area of the bottom (πr^2) +
- the area of the side $(2\pi r h)$.

Therefore without the top or bottom (lateral area), the surface area is

$$A = 2\pi r h.$$

With the top and bottom, the surface area is

$$A = 2\pi r^2 + 2\pi r h = 2\pi r(r + h).$$

For a given volume, the cylinder with the smallest surface area has h = 2r. For a given surface area, the cylinder with the largest volume has h = 2r, i.e. the cylinder fits in a cube (height = diameter.)

Cylindric sections are the intersections of cylinders with planes.

a. Right circular cylinder
c. 1-center problem
b. 2-3 heap
d. 120-cell

74. In mathematics, the _____s are analogs of the ordinary trigonometric functions. The basic _____s are the hyperbolic sine 'sinh', and the hyperbolic cosine 'cosh', from which are derived the hyperbolic tangent 'tanh', etc., in analogy to the derived trigonometric functions. The inverse _____ are the area hyperbolic sine 'arsinh' (also called 'asinh', or sometimes by the misnomer of 'arcsinh') and so on.

a. Heaviside step function
c. Rectangular function
b. Square root
d. Hyperbolic function

75. In common usage, a cylinder is taken to mean a finite section of a right _____ with its ends closed to form two circular surfaces, as in the figure (right.) If the cylinder has a radius r and length (height) h, then its volume is given by

$$V = \pi r^2 h$$

and its surface area is:

- the area of the top (πr^2) +
- the area of the bottom (πr^2) +
- the area of the side $(2\pi r h)$.

Therefore without the top or bottom (lateral area), the surface area is

$$A = 2\pi r h.$$

With the top and bottom, the surface area is

$$A = 2\pi r^2 + 2\pi r h = 2\pi r(r + h).$$

For a given volume, the cylinder with the smallest surface area has h = 2r. For a given surface area, the cylinder with the largest volume has h = 2r, i.e. the cylinder fits in a cube (height = diameter.)

Cylindric sections are the intersections of cylinders with planes.

a. 120-cell
b. 2-3 heap
c. 1-center problem
d. Circular Cylinder

76. In mathematics, specifically in topology, a _____ is a two-dimensional manifold. The most familiar examples are those that arise as the boundaries of solid objects in ordinary three-dimensional Euclidean space, EÂ³. On the other hand, there are also more exotic _____s, that are so 'contorted' that they cannot be embedded in three-dimensional space at all.
   a. Cross-cap
   b. Homoeoid
   c. Surface
   d. Standard torus

77. _____ is how much exposed area an object has. It is expressed in square units. If an object has flat faces, its _____ can be calculated by adding together the areas of its faces.
   a. Surface area
   b. Reflection group
   c. Compactness measure of a shape
   d. Relative dimension

78. A _____ is a symmetrical geometrical object. In non-mathematical usage, the term is used to refer either to a round ball or to its two-dimensional surface. In mathematics, a _____ is the set of all points in three-dimensional space which are at distance r from a fixed point of that space, where r is a positive real number called the radius of the _____.
   a. Lie derivative
   b. Differential geometry of curves
   c. Sphere
   d. Differentiable manifold

79. The _____ of an angle is the ratio of the length of the opposite side to the length of the hypotenuse. In our case

$$\sin A = \frac{\text{opposite}}{\text{hypotenuse}} = \frac{a}{h}.$$

Note that this ratio does not depend on size of the particular right triangle chosen, as long as it contains the angle A, since all such triangles are similar.

The cosine of an angle is the ratio of the length of the adjacent side to the length of the hypotenuse.

a. Right angle
b. Sine
c. Trigonometric functions
d. Law of sines

80. In trigonometry, the _____ is a function defined as tan x = $\sin x / \cos x$. The function is so-named because it can be defined as the length of a certain segment of a _____ (in the geometric sense) to the unit circle. In plane geometry, a line is _____ to a curve, at some point, if both line and curve pass through the point with the same direction.
a. Hopf conjectures
b. Projective connection
c. Conformal geometry
d. Tangent

81. _____ is a branch of mathematics that deals with triangles, particularly those plane triangles in which one angle has 90 degrees. _____ deals with relationships between the sides and the angles of triangles and with the trigonometric functions, which describe those relationships.

_____ has applications in both pure mathematics and in applied mathematics, where it is essential in many branches of science and technology.

a. Trigonometry
b. Trigonometric functions
c. Sine
d. Law of sines

82. _____ is an adjective meaning contiguous, adjoining or abutting.

In geometry, _____ is when sides meet to make an angle.

In trigonometry the _____ side of a right angled triangle is the cathetus next to the angle in question.

a. Ordered geometry
b. Affine geometry
c. Ambient space
d. Adjacent

83. In mathematics, the _____ of a number n is the number that, when added to n, yields zero. The _____ of n is denoted −n. For example, 7 is −7, because 7 + (−7) = 0, and the _____ of −0.3 is 0.3, because −0.3 + 0.3 = 0.
a. Additive inverse
b. Associativity
c. Arity
d. Algebraic structure

84. In statistics, the _____ is the value that occurs the most frequently in a data set or a probability distribution. In some fields, notably education, sample data are often called scores, and the sample _____ is known as the modal score.

Chapter 10. Geometry

Like the statistical mean and the median, the _____ is a way of capturing important information about a random variable or a population in a single quantity.

   a. Field
   c. Mode

   b. Deltoid
   d. Function

85. The Q-TIP of a geographic location is its height above a fixed reference point, often the mean sea level. _____, or geometric height, is mainly used when referring to points on the Earth's surface, while altitude or geopotential height is used for points above the surface, such as an aircraft in flight or a spacecraft in orbit.

Less commonly, _____ is measured using the center of the Earth as the reference point.

   a. A Mathematical Theory of Communication
   c. A chemical equation

   b. A posteriori
   d. Elevation

86. In mathematics, the _____ functions are functions of an angle; they are important when studying triangles and modeling periodic phenomena, among many other applications.
   a. Coversine
   c. Trigonometric

   b. Law of sines
   d. Gudermannian function

87. In mathematics and computer science, _____ is the study of graphs: mathematical structures used to model pairwise relations between objects from a certain collection. A 'graph' in this context refers to a collection of vertices or 'nodes' and a collection of edges that connect pairs of vertices. A graph may be undirected, meaning that there is no distinction between the two vertices associated with each edge, or its edges may be directed from one vertex to another; see graph for more detailed definitions and for other variations in the types of graphs that are commonly considered.
   a. Partial equivalence relation
   c. Discrete mathematics

   b. Graph theory
   d. Pooling design

88. A _____ is a structure built to span a gorge, valley, road, railroad track, river, body of water for the purpose of providing passage over the obstacle. Designs of _____s will vary depending on the function of the _____ and the nature of the terrain where the _____ is to be constructed. Roman _____ of Córdoba, Spain, built in the 1st century BC. Ponte di Pietra in Verona, Italy. A log _____ in the French Alps near Vallorcine. An English 18th century example of a _____ in the Palladian style, with shops on the span: Pulteney _____, Bath A Han Dynasty Chinese miniature model of two residential towers joined by a _____

The first _____s were made by nature -- as simple as a log fallen across a stream.

   a. Bridge
   c. 2-3 heap

   b. 1-center problem
   d. 120-cell

89. In graph theory, a _____ in a graph is a sequence of vertices such that from each of its vertices there is an edge to the next vertex in the sequence. The first vertex is called the start vertex and the last vertex is called the end vertex. Both of them are called end or terminal vertices of the _____.

Chapter 10. Geometry

a. Path
c. Class
b. Deltoid
d. Blinding

90. The word _____ has many distinct meanings in different fields of knowledge, depending on their methodologies and the context of discussion. Broadly speaking we can say that a _____ is some kind of belief or claim that (supposedly) explains, asserts, or consolidates some class of claims. Additionally, in contrast with a theorem the statement of the _____ is generally accepted only in some tentative fashion as opposed to regarding it as having been conclusively established.

a. Theory
c. Per mil
b. Transport of structure
d. Defined

91. _____ is the branch of mathematics that studies the properties of a space that are preserved under continuous deformations. _____ grew out of geometry, but unlike geometry, _____ is not concerned with metric properties such as distances between points. Instead, _____ involves the study of properties that describe how a space is assembled, such as connectedness and orientability.

a. Ring
c. Topology
b. 1-center problem
d. Structure

92. In mathematics, _____ has a few different, but closely related, meanings:

The _____ of a connected, orientable surface is an integer representing the maximum number of cuttings along closed simple curves without rendering the resultant manifold disconnected. It is equal to the number of handles on it. Alternatively, it can be defined in terms of the Euler characteristic χ, via the relationship χ = 2 − 2g for closed surfaces, where g is the _____.

a. Support vector machines
c. Skew
b. JPEG 2000
d. Genus

93. In the study of metric spaces in mathematics, there are various notions of two metrics on the same underlying space being 'the same', or _____.

In the following, M will denote a non-empty set and d_1 and d_2 will denote two metrics on M.

The two metrics d_1 and d_2 are said to be topologically _____ if they generate the same topology on M.

a. A Mathematical Theory of Communication
c. A posteriori
b. A chemical equation
d. Equivalent

94. In category theory, an abstract branch of mathematics, an _____ of a category C is an object I in C such that for every object X in C, there exists precisely one morphism I → X. The dual notion is that of a terminal object: T is terminal if for every object X in C there exists a single morphism X → T. _____s are also called coterminal, and terminal objects are also called final.

a. A Mathematical Theory of Communication
c. Initial object
b. A chemical equation
d. A posteriori

Chapter 10. Geometry

95. _____ is a non-Euclidean geometry, in which, given a line L and a point p outside L, there exists no line parallel to L passing through p.

_____, like hyperbolic geometry, violates Euclid's parallel postulate, which asserts that there is exactly one line parallel to L passing through p. In _____, there are no parallel lines at all.

a. Elliptic geometry
b. Erlangen Program
c. A Mathematical Theory of Communication
d. Adjacent angles

96. In mathematics, _____ is a non-Euclidean geometry, meaning that the parallel postulate of Euclidean geometry is replaced. The parallel postulate in Euclidean geometry states, in two dimensional space, for any given line l and point P not on l, there is exactly one line through P that does not intersect l;. In _____ there are at least two distinct lines through P which do not intersect l, so the parallel postulate is false.

a. Horocycle
b. Margulis lemma
c. Fuchsian group
d. Hyperbolic geometry

97. In mathematics, the _____ is a certain non-orientable surface, i.e., a surface with no distinct 'inner' and 'outer' sides. Other related non-orientable objects include the Möbius strip and the real projective plane. Whereas a Möbius strip is a two dimensional surface with boundary, a _____ has no boundary.

a. 1-center problem
b. 120-cell
c. 2-3 heap
d. Klein bottle

98. A _____ is a method for fastening or securing linear material such as rope by tying or interweaving. It may consist of a length of one or more segments of rope, string, webbing, twine, strap, or even chain interwoven such that the line can bind to itself or to some other object--the 'load'. _____s have been the subject of interest for their ancient origins, their common uses, and the mathematical implications of _____ theory.

a. 1-center problem
b. Knot
c. List of knots
d. Pretzel link

99. In mathematics, _____ is the area of topology that studies mathematical knots. While inspired by knots which appear in daily life in shoelaces and rope, a mathematician's knot differs drastically in that the ends are joined together to prevent it from becoming undone. In precise mathematical language, a knot is an embedding of a circle in 3-dimensional Euclidean space, R^3.

a. Ropelength
b. Homfly polynomial
c. Knot complement
d. Knot theory

100. In geometry, a _____ of radius R is a surface of curvature $-1/R^2$, by analogy with the sphere of radius R, which is a surface of curvature $1/R^2$. The term was introduced by Eugenio Beltrami in his 1868 paper on models of hyperbolic geometry.

The term is also used to refer to what is traditionally called a tractricoid: the result of revolving a tractrix about its asymptote, which is the subject of

It is a singular space, but away from the singularities, it has constant negative Gaussian curvature and therefore is locally isometric to a hyperbolic plane.

a. Round function
b. Systolic freedom
c. Tangent
d. Pseudosphere

101. Georg Friedrich Bernhard _____ was a German mathematician who made important contributions to analysis and differential geometry, some of them paving the way for the later development of general relativity.

_____ was born in Breselenz, a village near Dannenberg in the Kingdom of Hanover in what is today Germany. His father, Friedrich Bernhard _____, was a poor Lutheran pastor in Breselenz who fought in the Napoleonic Wars.

a. Brook Taylor
b. Paul C. van Oorschot
c. Gustave Bertrand
d. Riemann

102. In mathematics, the concept of a '_____' is used to describe the behavior of a function as its argument or input either 'gets close' to some point, or as the argument becomes arbitrarily large; or the behavior of a sequence's elements as their index increases indefinitely. _____s are used in calculus and other branches of mathematical analysis to define derivatives and continuity.

In formulas, _____ is usually abbreviated as lim.

a. Contact
b. Copula
c. Limit
d. Duality

103. _____ is a mathematical system attributed to the Greek mathematician Euclid of Alexandria. Euclid's Elements is the earliest known systematic discussion of geometry. It has been one of the most influential books in history, as much for its method as for its mathematical content.

a. Infinitely near point
b. Euclidean geometry
c. Equidimensional
d. Analytic geometry

104. A _____ is generally 'a rough or fragmented geometric shape that can be split into parts, each of which is a reduced-size copy of the whole,' a property called self-similarity. The term was coined by Benoît Mandelbrot in 1975 and was derived from the Latin fractus meaning 'broken' or 'fractured.' A mathematical _____ is based on an equation that undergoes iteration, a form of feedback based on recursion.

A _____ often has the following features:

- It has a fine structure at arbitrarily small scales.
- It is too irregular to be easily described in traditional Euclidean geometric language.
- It is self-similar.
- It has a Hausdorff dimension which is greater than its topological dimension.
- It has a simple and recursive definition.

Because they appear similar at all levels of magnification, _____s are often considered to be infinitely complex. Natural objects that approximate _____s to a degree include clouds, mountain ranges, lightning bolts, coastlines, and snow flakes.

a. Logical disjunction
b. Cube
c. Zero-point energy
d. Fractal

105. In mathematics, a self-similar object is exactly or approximately similar to a part of itself. Many objects in the real world, such as coastlines, are statistically self-similar: parts of them show the same statistical properties at many scales. _____ is a typical property of fractals.

a. Gravity set
b. Hausdorff dimension
c. Self-similarity
d. Cantor function

106. A _____ is a polyhedron composed of four triangular faces, three of which meet at each vertex. A regular _____ is one in which the four triangles are regular, or 'equilateral', and is one of the Platonic solids.

The _____ is one kind of pyramid, which is a polyhedron with a flat polygon base and triangular faces connecting the base to a common point.

a. 120-cell
b. 2-3 heap
c. 1-center problem
d. Tetrahedron

107. _____: A Romance of Many Dimensions is an 1884 science fiction novella by the English schoolmaster Edwin Abbott Abbott.

As a satire, _____ offered pointed observations on the social hierarchy of Victorian culture. However, the novella's more enduring contribution is its examination of dimensions; in a foreword to one of the many publications of the novella, noted science writer Isaac Asimov described _____ as 'The best introduction one can find into the manner of perceiving dimensions.' As such, the novella is still popular amongst mathematics, physics and computer science students.

a. 120-cell
b. 1-center problem
c. 2-3 heap
d. Flatland

108. _____ or the general theory of relativity is the geometric theory of gravitation published by Albert Einstein in 1916. It is the state-of-the art description of gravity in modern physics. It unifies special relativity and Newton's law of universal gravitation, and describes gravity as a property of the geometry of space and time, or spacetime.

a. Special relativity
b. General relativity
c. Presburger arithmetic
d. Peano axioms

Chapter 11. Counting Methods and Probability Theory

1. _____ is the noteworthy alignment of two or more events or circumstances without obvious causal connection. The word is derived from the Latin co- and incidere.

The index of _____ can be used to analyze whether two events are related.

a. 120-cell
b. 2-3 heap
c. Coincidence
d. 1-center problem

2. _____ is the likelihood or chance that something is the case or will happen. Theoretical _____ is used extensively in areas such as statistics, mathematics, science and philosophy to draw conclusions about the likelihood of potential events and the underlying mechanics of complex systems.

The word _____ does not have a consistent direct definition.

a. Standardized moment
b. Probability
c. Discrete random variable
d. Statistical significance

3. In set theory, a _____ is a partially ordered set such that for each t ∈ T, the set {s ∈ T : s < t} is well-ordered by the relation <. For each t ∈ T, the order type of {s ∈ T : s < t} is called the height of t. The height of T itself is the least ordinal greater than the height of each element of T.

a. Set-theoretic topology
b. Transitive reduction
c. Definable numbers
d. Tree

4. In mathematics, _____ and undefined are used to explain whether or not expressions have meaningful, sensible, and unambiguous values. Not all branches of mathematics come to the same conclusion.

The following expressions are undefined in all contexts, but remarks in the analysis section may apply.

a. LHS
b. Plugging in
c. Toy model
d. Defined

5. A _____ is a 2D geometric symbolic representation of information according to some visualization technique. Sometimes, the technique uses a 3D visualization which is then projected onto the 2D surface. The word graph is sometimes used as a synonym for _____.

a. 2-3 heap
b. 120-cell
c. 1-center problem
d. Diagram

6. In mathematics, a _____ is an algebraic structure consisting of a set together with an operation that combines any two of its elements to form a third element. To qualify as a _____, the set and operation must satisfy a few conditions called _____ axioms, namely associativity, identity and invertibility. While these are familiar from many mathematical structures, such as number systems--for example, the integers endowed with the addition operation form a _____--the formulation of the axioms is detached from the concrete nature of the _____ and its operation.

a. Coherence
b. Derivative algebra
c. Characteristic function
d. Group

7. A _____ is a form of gambling which involves the drawing of lots for a prize. Some governments outlaw it, while others endorse it to the extent of organizing a national _____. It is common to find some degree of regulation of _____ by governments.
   a. 120-cell
   b. 1-center problem
   c. 2-3 heap
   d. Lottery

8. In several fields of mathematics the term _____ is used with different but closely related meanings. They all relate to the notion of mapping the elements of a set to other elements of the same set, i.e., exchanging elements of a set.

The general concept of _____ can be defined more formally in different contexts:

In combinatorics, a _____ is usually understood to be a sequence containing each element from a finite set once, and only once.

   a. Linearly independent
   b. Cyclic permutation
   c. Permutation
   d. Tensor product

9. In mathematics, the _____ of a non-negative integer n, denoted by n!, is the product of all positive integers less than or equal to n. For example,

$$5! = 1 \times 2 \times 3 \times 4 \times 5 = 120$$

and
$$6! = 1 \times 2 \times 3 \times 4 \times 5 \times 6 = 720$$

The notation n! was introduced by Christian Kramp in 1808.

The _____ function is formally defined by

$$n! = \prod_{k=1}^{n} k \quad \forall n \in \mathbb{N}.$$

The above definition incorporates the instance

$$0! = 1$$

as an instance of the fact that the product of no numbers at all is 1.

   a. Plane partition
   b. Partition of a set
   c. Symbolic combinatorics
   d. Factorial

Chapter 11. Counting Methods and Probability Theory

10. A _____ typically refers to a class of handheld calculators that are capable of plotting graphs, solving simultaneous equations, and performing numerous other tasks with variables. Most popular _____s are also programmable, allowing the user to create customized programs, typically for scientific/engineering and education applications. Due to their large displays intended for graphing, they can also accommodate several lines of text and calculations at a time.
    a. Genus
    b. Bump mapping
    c. Support vector machines
    d. Graphing calculator

11. A _____ is a device for performing mathematical calculations, distinguished from a computer by having a limited problem solving ability and an interface optimized for interactive calculation rather than programming. _____s can be hardware or software, and mechanical or electronic, and are often built into devices such as PDAs or mobile phones.

    Modern electronic _____s are generally small, digital, and usually inexpensive.

    a. 1-center problem
    b. 2-3 heap
    c. 120-cell
    d. Calculator

12. In mathematics and in the sciences, a _____ (plural: _____e, formulæ or _____s) is a concise way of expressing information symbolically (as in a mathematical or chemical _____), or a general relationship between quantities. One of many famous _____e is Albert Einstein's $E = mc^2$ (see special relativity

    In mathematics, a _____ is a key to solve an equation with variables. For example, the problem of determining the volume of a sphere is one that requires a significant amount of integral calculus to solve.

    a. 120-cell
    b. 2-3 heap
    c. 1-center problem
    d. Formula

13. The _____ are the set of numbers consisting of the natural numbers including 0 and their negatives. They are numbers that can be written without a fractional or decimal component, and fall within the set {... −2, −1, 0, 1, 2, ...}.
    a. Integers
    b. A Mathematical Theory of Communication
    c. A posteriori
    d. A chemical equation

14. In combinatorial mathematics, a _____ is an un-ordered collection of distinct elements, usually of a prescribed size and taken from a given set. Given such a set S, a _____ of elements of S is just a subset of S, where as always forsets the order of the elements is not taken into account. Also, as always forsets, no elements can be repeated more than once in a _____; this is often referred to as a 'collection without repetition'.
    a. Sparsity
    b. Fill-in
    c. Heawood number
    d. Combination

15. In computational complexity theory, an algorithm is said to take _____ if the asymptotic upper bound for the time it requires is proportional to the size of the input, which is usually denoted n.

    Informally spoken, the running time increases linearly with the size of the input. For example, a procedure that adds up all elements of a list requires time proportional to the length of the list.

a. Time-constructible function
b. Constructible function
c. Truth table reduction
d. Linear time

16. In materials science, a _____ is a solid substance in which the atoms, molecules, or ions are arranged in an orderly repeating pattern extending in all three spatial dimensions.

The word _____ is a loan from the ancient Greek word κρῐ́σταλλος, which had the same meaning, but according to the ancient understanding of _____. At root it means anything congealed by freezing, such as ice.

a. 1-center problem
b. 120-cell
c. 2-3 heap
d. Crystal

17. A _____ is a dynamic set of visual, auditory, or tactile symbols of communication and the elements used to manipulate them. _____ can also refer to the use of such systems as a general phenomenon. Strictly speaking, _____ is considered to be an exclusively human mode of communication.

a. 1-center problem
b. 2-3 heap
c. Language
d. 120-cell

18. In probability theory, an _____ is a set of outcomes to which a probability is assigned. Typically, when the sample space is finite, any subset of the sample space is an _____. However, this approach does not work well in cases where the sample space is infinite, most notably when the outcome is a real number.

a. Information set
b. Equaliser
c. Audio compression
d. Event

19. In scientific inquiry, an _____ is a method of investigating particular types of research questions or solving particular types of problems. The _____ is a cornerstone in the empirical approach to acquiring deeper knowledge about the world and is used in both natural sciences as well as in social sciences. An _____ is defined, in science, as a method of investigating less known fields, solving practical problems and proving theoretical assumptions.

a. A chemical equation
b. A Mathematical Theory of Communication
c. Experiment
d. A posteriori

20. _____ is usually defined as the activity of using and developing computer technology, computer hardware and software. It is the computer-specific part of information technology. Computer science (or _____ science) is the study and the science of the theoretical foundations of information and computation and their implementation and application in computer systems.

a. Parallel Random Access Machine
b. Probabilistic Turing Machine
c. Deterministic finite state machine
d. Computing

21. The term _____ refers to the central sense organ complex, for those animals that have one, normally on the ventral surface of the head and can depending on the definition in the human case, include the hair, forehead, eyebrow, eyes, nose, ears, cheeks, mouth, lips, philtrum, teeth, skin, and chin. The _____ has uses of expression, appearance, and identity amongst others. It also has different senses like smelling, tasting, hearing, and seeing.

Chapter 11. Counting Methods and Probability Theory

Caricatures often exaggerate facial features to make a _____ more easily recognized in association with a pronounced portion of the _____ of the individual in question--for example, a caricature of Osama bin Laden might focus on his facial hair and nose; a caricature of George W. Bush might enlarge his ears to the size of an elephant¢s; a caricature of Jay Leno may pronounce his head and chin; and a caricature of Mick Jagger might enlarge his lips.

a. 1-center problem
b. 120-cell
c. Face
d. 2-3 heap

22. _____ , a discipline of biology, is the science of heredity and variation in living organisms. The fact that living things inherit traits from their parents has been used since prehistoric times to improve crop plants and animals through selective breeding. However, the modern science of _____, which seeks to understand the process of inheritance, only began with the work of Gregor Mendel in the mid-nineteenth century.

a. Polytomy
b. Fitness landscapes
c. Hardy-Weinberg principle
d. Genetics

23. The word _____ denotes information gained by means of observation, experience as opposed to theoretical. A central concept in science and the scientific method is that all evidence must be _____ that is, dependent on evidence or consequences that are observable by the senses. It is usually differentiated from the philosophic usage of empiricism by the use of the adjective '_____' or the adverb 'empirically.' '_____' as an adjective or adverb is used in conjunction with both the natural and social sciences, and refers to the use of working hypotheses that are testable using observation or experiment.

a. A chemical equation
b. A posteriori
c. Empirical
d. A Mathematical Theory of Communication

24. _____ or experimental probability, is the ratio of the number favorable outcomes to the total number of trials , not in a sample space but in an actual sequence of experiments. In a more general sense, _____ estimates probabilities from experience and observation. The phrase a posteriori probability has also been used an alternative to _____ or relative frequency.

a. A posteriori
b. Empirical probability
c. A Mathematical Theory of Communication
d. A chemical equation

25. In statistics, a _____ is an idealized randomizing device with two states which are equally likely to occur. It is based on the ubiquitous coin flip used in sports and other situations where it is necessary to give two parties the same chance of winning. Depending on the occasion a specially designed chip or a simple currency coin is used, which due to unequal weight distribution might be 'unfair': one state might occur more frequently than the other, giving one party an unfair advantage.

a. Medical statistics
b. Burr distribution
c. Count data
d. Fair coin

26. In mathematics and physics, there are a _____ number of topics named in honor of Leonhard Euler . As well, many of these topics include their own unique function, equation, formula, identity, number, or other mathematical entity. Unfortunately however, many of these entities have been given simple names like Euler's function, Euler's equation, and Euler's formula, which are further confused by variations of the 'Euler'-prefix Overall though, Euler's work touched upon so many fields that he is often the earliest written reference on a given matter.

a. List of trigonometry topics
b. List of integrals of logarithmic functions
c. List of mathematical knots and links
d. Large

27. In discrete mathematics and predominantly in set theory, a _____ is a concept used in comparisons of sets to refer to the unique values of one set in relation to another. The terms 'absolute' and 'relative' _____ refer to more specific applications of the concept, with universal _____s referring to elements unique to the universal set and the latter referring to the unique elements of one set in relation to another. In this image, the universal set is represented by the border of the image, and the set A as a disc.

a. Huge
b. Kernel
c. Derivative algebra
d. Complement

28. In simple terms, two events are _____ if they cannot occur at the same time.

In logic, two _____ propositions are propositions that logically cannot both be true. To say that more than two propositions are _____ may, depending on context mean that no two of them can both be true, or only that they cannot all be true.

a. Philosophy
b. Philosophy of mathematics
c. Determinism
d. Mutually exclusive

29. In probability theory and statistics the _____ in favour of an event or a proposition are the quantity p /, where p is the probability of the event or proposition. The _____ against the same event are / p. For example, if you chose a random day of the week, then the _____ that you would choose a Sunday would be 1/6, not 1/7.

a. Event
b. Anscombe transform
c. Estimation of covariance matrices
d. Odds

30. A _____ is a structured activity, usually undertaken for enjoyment and sometimes also used as an educational tool. _____s are distinct from work, which is usually carried out for remuneration, and from art, which is more concerned with the expression of ideas. However, the distinction is not clear-cut, and many _____s are also considered to be work (such as professional players of spectator sports/_____s) or art (such as jigsaw puzzles or _____s involving an artistic layout such as Mah-jongg solitaire.)

a. 120-cell
b. 1-center problem
c. Game
d. 2-3 heap

Chapter 11. Counting Methods and Probability Theory

31. The term _____ or centre is used in various contexts in abstract algebra to denote the set of all those elements that commute with all other elements. More specifically:

   - The _____ of a group G consists of all those elements x in G such that xg = gx for all g in G. This is a normal subgroup of G.
   - The _____ of a ring R is the subset of R consisting of all those elements x of R such that xr = rx for all r in R. The _____ is a commutative subring of R, so R is an algebra over its _____.
   - The _____ of an algebra A consists of all those elements x of A such that xa = ax for all a in A. See also: central simple algebra.
   - The _____ of a Lie algebra L consists of all those elements x in L such that [x,a] = 0 for all a in L. This is an ideal of the Lie algebra L.
   - The _____ of a monoidal category C consists of pairs *a natural isomorphism satisfying certain axioms.*

   a. Block size
   c. Disk
   b. Center
   d. Brute Force

32. _____ is the mathematical operation of scaling one number by another. It is one of the four basic operations in elementary arithmetic.

   _____ is defined for whole numbers in terms of repeated addition; for example, 4 multiplied by 3 can be calculated by adding 3 copies of 4 together:

   $$4 + 4 + 4 = 12.$$

   _____ of rational numbers and real numbers is defined by systematic generalization of this basic idea.

   a. The number 0 is even.
   c. Highest common factor
   b. Least common multiple
   d. Multiplication

33. _____ is the probability of some event A, given the occurrence of some other event B. _____ is written P[A | B], and is read 'the probability of A, given B'.

   Joint probability is the probability of two events in conjunction. That is, it is the probability of both events together. The joint probability of A and B is written $P(A \cap B)$ or $P(A,B)$.

   a. Renewal theory
   c. Quantile
   b. Sample space
   d. Conditional probability

34. In probability theory and statistics, the _____ of a random variable is the integral of the random variable with respect to its probability measure. For discrete random variables this is equivalent to the probability-weighted sum of the possible values, and for continuous random variables with a density function it is the probability density -weighted integral of the possible values.

   The _____ may be intuitively understood by the law of large numbers: The _____, when it exists, is almost surely the limit of the sample mean as sample size grows to infinity.

a. Expected value
b. Illustration
c. Event
d. Infinitely divisible distribution

35. A _____ is a software program that facilitates symbolic mathematics. The core functionality of a CAS is manipulation of mathematical expressions in symbolic form.

The symbolic manipulations supported typically include

- simplification to the smallest possible expression or some standard form, including automatic simplification with assumptions and simplification with constraints
- substitution of symbolic, functors or numeric values for expressions
- change of form of expressions: expanding products and powers, partial and full factorization, rewriting as partial fractions, constraint satisfaction, rewriting trigonometric functions as exponentials, etc.
- partial and total differentiation
- symbolic constrained and unconstrained global optimization
- solution of linear and some non-linear equations over various domains
- solution of some differential and difference equations
- taking some limits
- some indefinite and definite integration, including multidimensional integrals
- integral transforms
- arbitrary-precision numeric operations
- Series operations such as expansion, summation and products
- matrix operations including products, inverses, etc.
- display of mathematical expressions in two-dimensional mathematical form, often using typesetting systems similar to TeX
- add-ons for use in applied mathematics such as physics packages for physical computation
- plotting graphs and parametric plots of functions in two and three dimensions, and animating them
- APIs for linking it on an external program such as a database, or using in a programming language to use the _____
- drawing charts and diagrams
- string manipulation such as matching and searching
- statistical computation
- Theorem proving and verification
- graphic production and editing such as CGI and signal processing as image processing
- sound synthesis

Many also include a programming language, allowing users to implement their own algorithms.

Some _____s focus on a specific area of application; these are typically developed in academia and are free.

a. Computer algebra system
b. 1-center problem
c. 2-3 heap
d. 120-cell

Chapter 12. Statistics

1. A _____ is the result of applying a function to a set of data.

More formally, statistical theory defines a _____ as a function of a sample where the function itself is independent of the sample's distribution: the term is used both for the function and for the value of the function on a given sample.

A _____ is distinct from an unknown statistical parameter, which is not computable from a sample.

a. Statistic
b. Parameter space
c. Spatial dependence
d. Loss function

2. _____ is a mathematical science pertaining to the collection, analysis, interpretation or explanation, and presentation of data. It also provides tools for prediction and forecasting based on data. It is applicable to a wide variety of academic disciplines, from the natural and social sciences to the humanities, government and business.

a. Probability distribution
b. Regression toward the mean
c. Percentile rank
d. Statistics

3. _____ are used to describe the basic features of the data gathered from an experimental study in various ways. A _____ is distinguished from inductive statistics. They provide simple summaries about the sample and the measures.

a. Biostatistics
b. Null hypothesis
c. Failure rate
d. Descriptive statistics

4. In mathematics, _____ and undefined are used to explain whether or not expressions have meaningful, sensible, and unambiguous values. Not all branches of mathematics come to the same conclusion.

The following expressions are undefined in all contexts, but remarks in the analysis section may apply.

a. Toy model
b. Defined
c. LHS
d. Plugging in

5. In statistics, a _____ is a subset of a population. Typically, the population is very large, making a census or a complete enumeration of all the values in the population impractical or impossible. The _____ represents a subset of manageable size.

a. Dispersion
b. Duality
c. Boussinesq approximation
d. Sample

6. In signal processing, _____ is the reduction of a continuous signal to a discrete signal. A common example is the conversion of a sound wave to a sequence of samples.

A sample refers to a value or set of values at a point in time and/or space.

a. Disk
b. Decidable
c. Converse logic
d. Sampling

7. In statistics the _____ of an event i is the number n_i of times the event occurred in the experiment or the study. These frequencies are often graphically represented in histograms.

We speak of absolute frequencies, when the counts n_i themselves are given and of

$$f_i = \frac{n_i}{N} = \frac{n_i}{\sum_i n_i}$$

Taking the f_i for all i and tabulating or plotting them leads to a _____ distribution.

a. Frequency
b. Robinson-Dadson curves
c. Subharmonic
d. Digital room correction

8. In statistics, a _____ is a list of the values that a variable takes in a sample. It is usually a list, ordered by quantity, showing the number of times each value appears. For example, if 100 people rate a five-point Likert scale assessing their agreement with a statement on a scale on which 1 denotes strong agreement and 5 strong disagreement, the _____ of their responses might look like:

This simple tabulation has two drawbacks.

a. Percentile
b. Frequency distribution
c. Covariance
d. Confounding

9. In the fields of science, engineering, industry and statistics, _____ is the degree of closeness of a measured or calculated quantity to its actual value. _____ is closely related to precision, also called reproducibility or repeatability, the degree to which further measurements or calculations show the same or similar results. The results of calculations or a measurement can be accurate but not precise; precise but not accurate; neither; or both.

a. Accuracy
b. A Mathematical Theory of Communication
c. A posteriori
d. A chemical equation

10. In differential geometry, a discipline within mathematics, a _____ is a subset of the tangent bundle of a manifold satisfying certain properties. _____s are used to build up notions of integrability, and specifically of a foliation of a manifold

a. Discontinuity
b. Coherence
c. Constraint
d. Distribution

11. The _____ or Dirac's delta is a mathematical construct introduced by the British theoretical physicist Paul Dirac. Informally, it is a function representing an infinitely sharp peak bounding unit area: a function that has the value zero everywhere except at x = 0 where its value is infinitely large in such a way that its total integral is 1. It is a continuous analogue of the discrete Kronecker delta.

a. Hyperfunction
b. Schwartz kernel theorem
c. Weak derivative
d. Dirac delta

12. In set theory and its applications throughout mathematics, a _____ is a collection of sets that can be unambiguously defined by a property that all its members share. The precise definition of '_____' depends on foundational context. In work on ZF set theory, the notion of _____ is informal, whereas other set theories, such as NBG set theory, axiomatize the notion of '_____'.

a. Coherence	b. Class
c. Filter	d. Congruent

13. In geometry a _____ is traditionally a plane figure that is bounded by a closed path or circuit, composed of a finite sequence of straight line segments. These segments are called its edges or sides, and the points where two edges meet are the _____'s vertices or corners. The interior of the _____ is sometimes called its body.

a. Polygonal curve	b. Regular polygon
c. Polygon	d. Parallelogon

14. _____ are used in computer graphics to compose images that are three-dimensional in appearance. Usually triangular, _____ arise when an object's surface is modeled, vertices are selected, and the object is rendered in a wire frame model. This is quicker to display than a shaded model; thus the _____ are a stage in computer animation.

a. Polygons	b. Visibility polygon
c. Triskaidecagon	d. Heptadecagon

15. In mathematics, the concept of a '_____' is used to describe the behavior of a function as its argument or input either 'gets close' to some point, or as the argument becomes arbitrarily large; or the behavior of a sequence's elements as their index increases indefinitely. _____s are used in calculus and other branches of mathematical analysis to define derivatives and continuity.

In formulas, _____ is usually abbreviated as lim.

a. Contact	b. Limit
c. Duality	d. Copula

16. In mathematics, a _____ of a set S in a topological space X is a point x in X that can be 'approximated' by points of S other than x itself. This concept profitably generalizes the notion of a limit and is the underpinning of concepts such as closed set and topological closure. Indeed, a set is closed if and only if it contains all of its _____s, and the topological closure operation can be thought of as an operation that enriches a set by adding its _____s.

a. Limit point	b. 2-3 heap
c. 120-cell	d. 1-center problem

17. A bar chart or _____ is a chart with rectangular bars with lengths proportional to the values that they represent. Bar charts are used for comparing two or more values. The bars can be horizontally or vertically oriented.

a. 120-cell	b. 2-3 heap
c. 1-center problem	d. Bar graph

18. In statistics, a _____ is a graphical display of tabulated frequencies, shown as bars. It shows what proportion of cases fall into each of several categories. A _____ differs from a bar chart in that it is the area of the bar that denotes the value, not the height as in bar charts, a crucial distinction when the categories are not of uniform width.

a. Probability distribution	b. Standardized moment
c. First-hitting-time models	d. Histogram

19. In a graph theory, the _____ L

One of the earliest and most important theorems about _____s is due to Hassler Whitney, who proved that with one exceptional case the structure of G can be recovered completely from its _____.

a. Sparse graph
b. Bivariegated graph
c. Vertex-transitive graph
d. Line graph

20. In graph theory, a _____ in a graph is a sequence of vertices such that from each of its vertices there is an edge to the next vertex in the sequence. The first vertex is called the start vertex and the last vertex is called the end vertex. Both of them are called end or terminal vertices of the _____.

a. Blinding
b. Class
c. Path
d. Deltoid

21. A _____ is is a graphical technique for presenting a data set drawn by hand or produced by a mechanical or electronic plotter. It is a graph depicting the relationship between two or more variables used, for instance, in visualising scientific data.

_____s play an important role in statistics and data analysis.

a. C-35
b. Lattice
c. Plot
d. Dini

22. In botany, a _____ is an above-ground plant organ specialized for photosynthesis. For this purpose, a _____ is typically flat and thin, to expose the cells containing chloroplast to light over a broad area, and to allow light to penetrate fully into the tissues. Leaves are also the sites in most plants where transpiration and guttation take place.

a. 2-3 heap
b. 120-cell
c. 1-center problem
d. Leaf

23. In mathematics, an _____, or central tendency of a data set refers to a measure of the 'middle' or 'expected' value of the data set. There are many different descriptive statistics that can be chosen as a measurement of the central tendency of the data items.

An _____ is a single value that is meant to typify a list of values.

a. A posteriori
b. A Mathematical Theory of Communication
c. A chemical equation
d. Average

24. In mathematics, an average, or _____ of a data set refers to a measure of the 'middle' or 'expected' value of the data set. There are many different descriptive statistics that can be chosen as a measurement of the _____ of the data items.

An average is a single value that is meant to typify a list of values.

a. Trimean
b. Quartile
c. Mean reciprocal rank
d. Central tendency

25. In mathematics the concept of a _____ generalizes notions such as 'length', 'area', and 'volume'. Informally, given some base set, a '_____' is any consistent assignment of 'sizes' to the subsets of the base set. Depending on the application, the 'size' of a subset may be interpreted as its physical size, the amount of something that lies within the subset, or the probability that some random process will yield a result within the subset.

 a. Cusp
 b. Lattice
 c. Measure
 d. Congruent

26. In statistics, _____ has two related meanings:

- the arithmetic _____.
- the expected value of a random variable, which is also called the population _____.

It is sometimes stated that the '_____' _____s average. This is incorrect if '_____' is taken in the specific sense of 'arithmetic _____' as there are different types of averages: the _____, median, and mode. For instance, average house prices almost always use the median value for the average.

For a real-valued random variable X, the _____ is the expectation of X.

 a. Mean
 b. Statistical population
 c. Probability
 d. Proportional hazards model

27. _____ is the addition of a set of numbers; the result is their sum or total. An interim or present total of a _____ process is termed the running total. The 'numbers' to be summed may be natural numbers, complex numbers, matrices, or still more complicated objects.

 a. Summation
 b. 120-cell
 c. 2-3 heap
 d. 1-center problem

28. A calculation is a deliberate process for transforming one or more inputs into one or more results, with variable change.

The term is used in a variety of senses, from the very definite arithmetical using an algorithm to the vague heuristics of _____ a strategy in a competition or _____ the chance of a successful relationship between two people.

Multiplying 7 by 8 is a simple algorithmic calculation.

 a. Calculation
 b. Calculating
 c. Mathematics Subject Classification
 d. Mathematical maturity

29. In geometry, a _____ of a triangle is a line segment joining a vertex to the midpoint of the opposing side. Every triangle has exactly three _____s; one running from each vertex to the opposite side.

The three _____s are concurrent at a point known as the triangle's centroid, or center of mass of the triangle.

a. Statistical significance
c. Percentile rank
b. Median
d. Correlation

30. In statistics, the mid-range or mid-extreme of a set of statistical data values is the arithmetic mean of the maximum and minimum values in a data set, or:

$$\frac{\max x + \min x}{2}.$$

As such it is a measure of central tendency.

The _____ is highly sensitive to outliers and ignores all but two data points. It is therefore a very non-robust statistic, and it is rarely used in statistical analysis.

a. Midrange
c. Mean of circular quantities
b. Weighted mean
d. Geometric-harmonic mean

31. In statistics, the _____ is the value that occurs the most frequently in a data set or a probability distribution. In some fields, notably education, sample data are often called scores, and the sample _____ is known as the modal score.

Like the statistical mean and the median, the _____ is a way of capturing important information about a random variable or a population in a single quantity.

a. Deltoid
c. Field
b. Mode
d. Function

32. A _____ is a collection of data, usually presented in tabular form. Each column represents a particular variable. Each row corresponds to a given member of the _____ in question.

a. 120-cell
c. Data set
b. 2-3 heap
d. 1-center problem

33. The _____ is similar to an arithmetic mean, where instead of each of the data points contributing equally to the final average, some data points contribute more than others. The notion of _____ plays a role in descriptive statistics and also occurs in a more general form in several other areas of mathematics.

If all the weights are equal, then the _____ is the same as the arithmetic mean.

a. Mid-range
c. Quasi-arithmetic mean
b. Weighted mean
d. Truncated mean

34. In optics, _____ is the phenomenon in which the phase velocity of a wave depends on its frequency. Media having such a property are termed dispersive media.

The most familiar example of _____ is probably a rainbow, in which _____ causes the spatial separation of a white light into components of different wavelengths.

a. Crib
c. Depth
b. Boussinesq approximation
d. Dispersion

35. In descriptive statistics, the _____ is the length of the smallest interval which contains all the data. It is calculated by subtracting the smallest observations from the greatest and provides an indication of statistical dispersion.

It is measured in the same units as the data.

a. Kernel
c. Class
b. Bandwidth
d. Range

36. In statistics, the _____ of an element of a data set is the absolute difference between that element and a given point. Typically the point from which the deviation is measured is the value of either the median or the mean of the data set.

$$|D| = |x_i - m½|$$

where

$|D|$ is the _____,
x_i is the data element
and m is the chosen measure of central tendency of the data set--sometimes the mean, but most often the median.

a. Absolute deviation
c. Interquartile range
b. A Mathematical Theory of Communication
d. A chemical equation

37. In probability and statistics, the _____ is a measure of the dispersion of a collection of numbers. It can apply to a probability distribution, a random variable, a population or a data set. The _____ is usually denoted with the letter σ.
a. Statistical population
c. Standard deviation
b. Failure rate
d. Null hypothesis

38. In mathematics and statistics, _____ is a measure of difference for interval and ratio variables between the observed value and the mean. The sign of _____, either positive or negative, indicates whether the observation is larger than or smaller than the mean. The magnitude of the value reports how different an observation is from the mean.
a. Filter
c. Functional
b. Conchoid
d. Deviation

39. _____ is usually defined as the activity of using and developing computer technology, computer hardware and software. It is the computer-specific part of information technology. Computer science (or _____ science) is the study and the science of the theoretical foundations of information and computation and their implementation and application in computer systems.

Chapter 12. Statistics

a. Probabilistic Turing Machine
b. Deterministic finite state machine
c. Computing
d. Parallel Random Access Machine

40. In mathematics, specifically in combinatorial commutative algebra, a convex lattice polytope P is called _____ if it has the following property: given any positive integer n, every lattice point of the dilation nP, obtained from P by scaling its vertices by the factor n and taking the convex hull of the resulting points, can be written as the sum of exactly n lattice points in P. This property plays an important role in the theory of toric varieties, where it corresponds to projective normality of the toric variety determined by P.

The simplex in R^k with the vertices at the origin and along the unit coordinate vectors is _____.

a. Hypercube
b. Normal
c. Demihypercubes
d. Polytetrahedron

41. The _____ is an important family of continuous probability distributions, applicable in many fields. Each member of the family may be defined by two parameters, location and scale: the mean and variance respectively. The standard _____ is the _____ with a mean of zero and a variance of one.

a. Null hypothesis
b. Normal distribution
c. Percentile rank
d. Coefficient of variation

42. A _____ is a type of affix attached to a stem which modifies the meaning of that stem.

The word '_____' is itself made up of the stem fix, and the _____ pre-, both of which are derived from Latin roots.

- English _____ es
- _____ es and suffixes in Hebrew

a. 1-center problem
b. 2-3 heap
c. Prefix
d. 120-cell

43. _____ is a dimensionless quantity derived by subtracting the population mean from an individual raw score and then dividing the difference by the population standard deviation.

a. Z-score
b. 2-3 heap
c. 1-center problem
d. 120-cell

44. A _____ is the value of a variable below which a certain percent of observations fall. So the 20th _____ is the value below which 20 percent of the observations may be found. The term _____ and the related term _____ rank are often used in descriptive statistics as well as in the reporting of scores from norm-referenced tests.

a. Frequency distribution
b. Logistic regression
c. Statistically significant
d. Percentile

45. In descriptive statistics, a _____ is any of the three values which divide the sorted data set into four equal parts, so that each part represents one fourth of the sampled population.

- first _____ = lower _____ = cuts off lowest 25% of data = 25th percentile
- second _____ = median = cuts data set in half = 50th percentile
- third _____ = upper _____ = cuts off highest 25% of data, or lowest 75% = 75th percentile

The difference between the upper and lower _____s is called the interquartile range.

There is no universal agreement on choosing the _____ values.

The formula for the position of the observation at a given percentile, y, with n data points sorted in ascending order is:

$$L_y = (n+1)\left(\frac{y}{100}\right)$$

Example 4.
- a. Trimean
- b. Mean reciprocal rank
- c. Seven-number summary
- d. Quartile

46. In statistics, a standard score is a dimensionless quantity derived by subtracting the population mean from an individual raw score and then dividing the difference by the population standard deviation. This conversion process is called standardizing or normalizing.

Standard scores are also called z-values, _____, normal scores, and standardized variables.

- a. Bernstein inequalities
- b. Z-scores
- c. CIE 1931 XYZ color space
- d. Converge absolutely

47. The _____ is a statistic expressing the amount of random sampling error in a survey's results. The larger the _____, the less faith one should have that the poll's reported results are close to the 'true' figures; that is, the figures for the whole population.

The _____ is usually defined as the 'radius' of a confidence interval for a particular statistic from a survey.

- a. Moment about the mean
- b. Conditional variance
- c. Margin of error
- d. Squared deviations

48. In probability theory and statistics, _____ indicates the strength and direction of a linear relationship between two random variables. That is in contrast with the usage of the term in colloquial speech, denoting any relationship, not necessarily linear. In general statistical usage, _____ or co-relation refers to the departure of two random variables from independence.

a. Correlation
b. Sample size
c. Random variables
d. Summary statistics

49. In mathematics, a _____ on a fiber bundle is a device that defines a notion of parallel transport on the bundle; that is, a way to 'connect' or identify fibers over nearby points. If the fiber bundle is a vector bundle, then the notion of parallel transport is required to be linear. Such a _____ is equivalently specified by a covariant derivative, which is an operator that can differentiate sections of that bundle along tangent directions in the base manifold.
   a. 120-cell
   b. Connectivity
   c. 1-center problem
   d. Connection

50. In mathematics, the _____ is a way of specifying a derivative along tangent vectors of a manifold. Alternatively, the _____ is a way of introducing and working with a connection on a manifold by means of a differential operator, to be contrasted with the approach given by a principal connection on the frame bundle -- see Affine connection
   a. Lie derivative
   b. Covariant derivative
   c. Minimal surface
   d. Tractor bundle

51. A _____ is a type of display using Cartesian coordinates to display values for two variables for a set of data. The data is displayed as a collection of points, each having the value of one variable determining the position on the horizontal axis and the value of the other variable determining the position on the vertical axis. A _____ is also called a scatter chart, scatter diagram and scatter graph.
   a. 120-cell
   b. 1-center problem
   c. 2-3 heap
   d. Scatter plot

52. In mathematics, in the realm of group theory, a group is said to be _____ if it equals its own commutator subgroup if the group has no nontrivial abelian quotients.

The smallest _____ group is the alternating group A_5. More generally, any non-abelian simple group is _____ since the commutator subgroup is a normal subgroup with abelian quotient.

   a. Free product
   b. Quaternion group
   c. Perfect
   d. Group of Lie type

53. The _____ fallacy is an informal fallacy. It ascribes cause where none exists. The flaw is failing to account for natural fluctuations.
   a. Depth
   b. Degrees of freedom
   c. Differential
   d. Regression

54. In mathematics, a _____ is a constant multiplicative factor of a certain object. For example, in the expression $9x^2$, the _____ of x^2 is 9.

The object can be such things as a variable, a vector, a function, etc.

   a. Stability radius
   b. Multivariate division algorithm
   c. Fibonacci polynomials
   d. Coefficient

55. In mathematics, the _____ is an approach to finding a particular solution to certain inhomogeneous ordinary differential equations and recurrence relations. It is closely related to the annihilator method, but instead of using a particular kind of differential operator in order to find the best possible form of the particular solution, a 'guess' is made as to the appropriate form, which is then tested by differentiating the resulting equation. In this sense, the _____ is less formal but more intuitive than the annihilator method.
- a. Differential algebraic equations
- b. Phase line
- c. Linear differential equation
- d. Method of undetermined coefficients

56. A _____ typically refers to a class of handheld calculators that are capable of plotting graphs, solving simultaneous equations, and performing numerous other tasks with variables. Most popular _____s are also programmable, allowing the user to create customized programs, typically for scientific/engineering and education applications. Due to their large displays intended for graphing, they can also accommodate several lines of text and calculations at a time.
- a. Support vector machines
- b. Bump mapping
- c. Genus
- d. Graphing calculator

57. A _____ is a device for performing mathematical calculations, distinguished from a computer by having a limited problem solving ability and an interface optimized for interactive calculation rather than programming. _____s can be hardware or software, and mechanical or electronic, and are often built into devices such as PDAs or mobile phones.

Modern electronic _____s are generally small, digital, and usually inexpensive.

- a. 120-cell
- b. 2-3 heap
- c. Calculator
- d. 1-center problem

58. In combinatorial mathematics, a _____ is an un-ordered collection of distinct elements, usually of a prescribed size and taken from a given set. Given such a set S, a _____ of elements of S is just a subset of S, where as always forsets the order of the elements is not taken into account. Also, as always forsets, no elements can be repeated more than once in a _____; this is often referred to as a 'collection without repetition'.
- a. Fill-in
- b. Heawood number
- c. Sparsity
- d. Combination

59. The _____ are the set of numbers consisting of the natural numbers including 0 and their negatives. They are numbers that can be written without a fractional or decimal component, and fall within the set {... −2, −1, 0, 1, 2, ...}.
- a. A chemical equation
- b. Integers
- c. A posteriori
- d. A Mathematical Theory of Communication

60. _____ In statistics, a result is called statistically significant if it is unlikely to have occurred by chance. "A statistically significant difference" simply means there is statistical evidence that there is a difference; it does not mean the difference is necessarily large, important, or significant in the common meaning of the word.
- a. Survival analysis
- b. Confounding
- c. Statistical significance
- d. Variance

Chapter 13. Mathematical Systems

1. In mathematics, a _____ is a calculation involving two operands, in other words, an operation whose arity is two. _____s can be accomplished using either a binary function or binary operator. _____s are sometimes called dyadic operations in order to avoid confusion with the binary numeral system.
   a. Binary operation
   b. 120-cell
   c. 1-center problem
   d. 2-3 heap

2. In mathematics, _____ and undefined are used to explain whether or not expressions have meaningful, sensible, and unambiguous values. Not all branches of mathematics come to the same conclusion.

   The following expressions are undefined in all contexts, but remarks in the analysis section may apply.

   a. Plugging in
   b. Toy model
   c. LHS
   d. Defined

3. In topology and related branches of mathematics, a _____ is a set whose complement is open.
   a. Coherent topology
   b. Cocountable topology
   c. Wallman compactification
   d. Closed set

4. In mathematics, a set is said to be _____ if the operation on members of the set produces a member of the set. For example, the real numbers are closed under subtraction, but the natural numbers are not: 3 and 7 are both natural numbers, but the result of 3 − 7 is not.

   Similarly, a set is said to be closed under a collection of operations if it is closed under each of the operations individually.

   a. Contingency table
   b. Closed under some operation
   c. Continuous linear extension
   d. Control chart

5. _____ or set diagrams are diagrams that show all hypothetically possible logical relations between a finite collection of sets. _____ were invented around 1880 by John Venn. They are used in many fields, including set theory, probability, logic, statistics, and computer science.
   a. 2-3 heap
   b. 120-cell
   c. Venn diagrams
   d. 1-center problem

6. In mathematics, _____ is a property that a binary operation can have. It means that, within an expression containing two or more of the same associative operators in a row, the order that the operations are performed does not matter as long as the sequence of the operands is not changed. That is, rearranging the parentheses in such an expression will not change its value.
   a. Idempotence
   b. Algebraically closed
   c. Associativity
   d. Unital

7. A _____ is a 2D geometric symbolic representation of information according to some visualization technique. Sometimes, the technique uses a 3D visualization which is then projected onto the 2D surface. The word graph is sometimes used as a synonym for _____.
   a. 2-3 heap
   b. 120-cell
   c. Diagram
   d. 1-center problem

8. The _____ is a rule which states that when you add or multiply numbers, changing the order doesn't change the result.
   a. Coimage
   b. Semigroupoid
   c. Conditional event algebra
   d. Commutative law

9. In mathematics, the term _____ has several different important meanings:

   - An _____ is an equality that remains true regardless of the values of any variables that appear within it, to distinguish it from an equality which is true under more particular conditions. For this, the 'triple bar' symbol ≡ is sometimes used.
   - In algebra, an _____ or _____ element of a set S with a binary operation Â· is an element e that, when combined with any element x of S, produces that same x. That is, eÂ·x = xÂ·e = x for all x in S.
     - The _____ function from a set S to itself, often denoted id or id_S, s the function such that i = x for all x in S. This function serves as the _____ element in the set of all functions from S to itself with respect to function composition.
     - In linear algebra, the _____ matrix of size n is the n-by-n square matrix with ones on the main diagonal and zeros elsewhere. This matrix serves as the _____ with respect to matrix multiplication.

A common example of the first meaning is the trigonometric _____

$$\sin^2\theta + \cos^2\theta = 1$$

which is true for all real values of θ, as opposed to

$$\cos\theta = 1,$$

which is true only for some values of θ, not all. For example, the latter equation is true when $\theta = 0$, false when $\theta = 2$

The concepts of 'additive _____' and 'multiplicative _____' are central to the Peano axioms. The number 0 is the 'additive _____' for integers, real numbers, and complex numbers. For the real numbers, for all $a \in \mathbb{R}$,

$$0 + a = a,$$

$$a + 0 = a,\text{ and}$$

$$0 + 0 = 0.$$

Similarly, The number 1 is the 'multiplicative _____' for integers, real numbers, and complex numbers.

a. Intersection
b. ARIA
c. Action
d. Identity

10. In mathematics, an _____ is a special type of element of a set with respect to a binary operation on that set. It leaves other elements unchanged when combined with them. This is used for groups and related concepts.
    a. Universal algebra
    b. Arity
    c. Identity element
    d. Algebraically closed

11. In mathematics, an _____ or member of a set is any one of the distinct objects that make up that set.

    Writing A = {1,2,3,4}, means that the _____s of the set A are the numbers 1, 2, 3 and 4. Groups of _____s of A, for example {1,2}, are subsets of A.

    a. Order
    b. Universal code
    c. Ideal
    d. Element

12. _____ is the mathematical operation of scaling one number by another. It is one of the four basic operations in elementary arithmetic.

    _____ is defined for whole numbers in terms of repeated addition; for example, 4 multiplied by 3 can be calculated by adding 3 copies of 4 together:

    $$4 + 4 + 4 = 12.$$

    _____ of rational numbers and real numbers is defined by systematic generalization of this basic idea.

    a. Highest common factor
    b. Least common multiple
    c. The number 0 is even.
    d. Multiplication

13. In mathematics, the _____ of a number n is the number that, when added to n, yields zero. The _____ of n is denoted −n. For example, 7 is −7, because 7 + (−7) = 0, and the _____ of −0.3 is 0.3, because −0.3 + 0.3 = 0.
    a. Additive inverse
    b. Algebraic structure
    c. Arity
    d. Associativity

14. In mathematics, a _____ is a number which can be expressed as a ratio of two integers. Non-integer _____s are usually written as the vulgar fraction $\frac{a}{b}$, where b is not zero. a is called the numerator, and b the denominator.
    a. Rational number
    b. Tally marks
    c. Minkowski distance
    d. Pre-algebra

15. In mathematics, the multiplicative inverse of a number x, denoted 1/x or x^{-1}, is the number which, when multiplied by x, yields 1. The multiplicative inverse of x is also called the _____ of x.
    a. 120-cell
    b. 2-3 heap
    c. Reciprocal
    d. 1-center problem

Chapter 13. Mathematical Systems

16. In mathematics, an _____ is a statement about the relative size or order of two objects, or about whether they are the same or not

- The notation a < b means that a is less than b.
- The notation a > b means that a is greater than b.
- The notation a ≠ b means that a is not equal to b, but does not say that one is bigger than the other or even that they can be compared in size.

In all these cases, a is not equal to b, hence, '_____'.

These relations are known as strict _____

- The notation a ≤ b means that a is less than or equal to b;
- The notation a ≥ b means that a is greater than or equal to b;

An additional use of the notation is to show that one quantity is much greater than another, normally by several orders of magnitude.

- The notation a << b means that a is much less than b.
- The notation a >> b means that a is much greater than b.

If the sense of the _____ is the same for all values of the variables for which its members are defined, then the _____ is called an 'absolute' or 'unconditional' _____. If the sense of an _____ holds only for certain values of the variables involved, but is reversed or destroyed for other values of the variables, it is called a conditional _____.

An _____ may appear unsolvable because it only states whether a number is larger or smaller than another number; but it is possible to apply the same operations for equalities to inequalities. For example, to find x for the _____ 10x > 23 one would divide 23 by 10.

a. A posteriori
b. A Mathematical Theory of Communication
c. A chemical equation
d. Inequality

17. The _____ is a decimalised system of measurement. It exists in several variations, with different choices of base units, though the choice of base units does not affect its day-to-day use. Over the last two centuries, different variants have been considered the _____.

a. 1-center problem
b. George Dantzig
c. Nonlinear system
d. Metric system

18. _____ generally conveys two primary meanings. The first is an imprecise sense of harmonious or aesthetically-pleasing proportionality and balance; such that it reflects beauty or perfection. The second meaning is a precise and well-defined concept of balance or 'patterned self-similarity' that can be demonstrated or proved according to the rules of a formal system: by geometry, through physics or otherwise.

a. Molecular symmetry
b. Symmetry breaking
c. Symmetry
d. Tessellation

19. _____ is a quantity expressing the two-dimensional size of a defined part of a surface, typically a region bounded by a closed curve. The term surface _____ refers to the total _____ of the exposed surface of a 3-dimensional solid, such as the sum of the _____s of the exposed sides of a polyhedron. _____ is an important invariant in the differential geometry of surfaces.
a. A Mathematical Theory of Communication
b. A posteriori
c. Area
d. A chemical equation

20. Generally speaking, an object with _____ is an object that looks the same after a certain amount of rotation. An object may have more than one _____; for instance, if reflections or turning it over are not counted, the triskelion appearing on the Isle of Man's flag has three rotational symmetries. More examples may be seen below.
a. 1-center problem
b. 120-cell
c. 2-3 heap
d. Rotational Symmetry

21. In mathematics, a _____ is an algebraic structure consisting of a set together with an operation that combines any two of its elements to form a third element. To qualify as a _____, the set and operation must satisfy a few conditions called _____ axioms, namely associativity, identity and invertibility. While these are familiar from many mathematical structures, such as number systems--for example, the integers endowed with the addition operation form a _____--the formulation of the axioms is detached from the concrete nature of the _____ and its operation.
a. Coherence
b. Characteristic function
c. Group
d. Derivative algebra

22. In set theory, a _____ is a partially ordered set such that for each t ∈ T, the set {s ∈ T : s < t} is well-ordered by the relation <. For each t ∈ T, the order type of {s ∈ T : s < t} is called the height of t. The height of T itself is the least ordinal greater than the height of each element of T.
a. Definable numbers
b. Tree
c. Set-theoretic topology
d. Transitive reduction

23. In cryptography, the _____ was a method devised by Polish mathematician-cryptologist Jerzy RóÅ¼ycki, at the Polish General Staff's Cipher Bureau, to facilitate decrypting German Enigma messages. This method sometimes made it possible to determine which of the Enigma machine's rotors was at the far right, that is, in the position where the rotor always revolved at every depression of a key.

- Biuro Szyfrów

a. FROSTBURG
b. Clock
c. Bombe
d. TWIRL

24. In mathematics, _____ is a system of arithmetic for integers, where numbers 'wrap around' after they reach a certain value -- the modulus. _____ was introduced by Carl Friedrich Gauss in his book Disquisitiones Arithmeticae, published in 1801.

A familiar use of _____ is its use in the 24-hour clock: the arithmetic of time-keeping in which the day runs from midnight to midnight and is divided into 24 hours, numbered from 0 to 23.

a. Residue number system
b. Discrete logarithm
c. Multiplicative group of integers modulo n
d. Modular arithmetic

25. As an abstract term, _____ means similarity between objects.
a. 120-cell
b. 1-center problem
c. Congruence
d. 2-3 heap

26. The word _____ is the Latin ablative of modulus which itself means 'a small measure.' It was introduced into mathematics in the book Disquisitiones Arithmeticae by Carl Friedrich Gauss in 1801. Ever since, however, '_____' has gained many meanings, some exact and some imprecise.

- (This usage is from Gauss's book.) Given the integers a, b and n, the expression a ≡ b (mod n) means that a − b is a multiple of n, or equivalently, a and b both leave the same remainder when divided by n. For more details, see modular arithmetic.

- In computing, given two numbers (either integer or real), a and n, a _____ n is the remainder after numerical division of a by n, under certain constraints. See _____ operation.

a. Quotition
b. Per mil
c. Predictor-corrector method
d. Modulo

27. In information theory, a _____ is a function mapping an alphabet to non-negative real numbers, satisfying a generalization of Kraft's inequality. A _____ page, a type of character encoding table, is one such _____.
a. Link encryption
b. File Camouflage
c. Code
d. Deterministic encryption

28. The _____ is a unique, numerical commercial book identifier, based upon the 9-digit Standard Book Numbering code created in the UK by the booksellers and stationers W.H. Smith and others in 1966. The 10-digit _____ format was developed by the International Organization for Standardization and published as an international standard, ISO 2108, in 1970. Currently, the ISO TC 46/SC 9 is responsible for the standard.
a. A Mathematical Theory of Communication
b. A posteriori
c. A chemical equation
d. ISBN

29. The _____ is a barcode symbology, that is widely used in the United States and Canada for tracking trade items in stores. In the _____-A barcode, each digit is represented by a seven-bit sequence, encoded by a series of alternating bars and spaces. Guard bars, shown in green, separate the two groups of six digits.

The _____ encodes 12 decimal digits as SLLLLLLMRRRRRRE, where S and E are the bit pattern 101, M is the bit pattern 01010, and each L and R are digits, each one represented by a seven-bit code.

a. A Mathematical Theory of Communication
b. A posteriori
c. A chemical equation
d. Universal product code

Chapter 14. Voting and Apportionment

1. In logic and philosophy, _____ refers to either (a) the 'content' or 'meaning' of a meaningful declarative sentence or (b) the pattern of symbols, marks, or sounds that make up a meaningful declarative sentence. _____s in either case are intended to be truth-bearers, that is, they are either true or false.

   The existence of _____s in the former sense, as well as the existence of 'meanings', is disputed.

   a. Laws of classical logic
   b. Proposition
   c. Linear logic
   d. Logicism

2. The _____ is a single-winner election method in which voters rank candidates in order of preference. The _____ determines the winner of an election by giving each candidate a certain number of points corresponding to the position in which he or she is ranked by each voter. Once all votes have been counted the candidate with the most points is the winner.

   a. 1-center problem
   b. 120-cell
   c. 2-3 heap
   d. Borda count

3. An _____ is a decision-making process by which a population chooses an individual to hold formal office. This is the usual mechanism by which modern democracy fills offices in the legislature, sometimes in the executive and judiciary, and for regional and local government. This process is also used in many other private and business organizations, from clubs to voluntary associations and corporations.

   a. Election
   b. A chemical equation
   c. A posteriori
   d. A Mathematical Theory of Communication

4. A _____ is a structured activity, usually undertaken for enjoyment and sometimes also used as an educational tool. _____s are distinct from work, which is usually carried out for remuneration, and from art, which is more concerned with the expression of ideas. However, the distinction is not clear-cut, and many _____s are also considered to be work (such as professional players of spectator sports/_____s) or art (such as jigsaw puzzles or _____s involving an artistic layout such as Mah-jongg solitaire.)

   a. 2-3 heap
   b. Game
   c. 1-center problem
   d. 120-cell

5. In mathematics, a _____ is a statement that can be proved on the basis of explicitly stated or previously agreed assumptions.

   a. Logical value
   b. Boolean function
   c. Theorem
   d. Disjunction introduction

6. The word _____ has many distinct meanings in different fields of knowledge, depending on their methodologies and the context of discussion. Broadly speaking we can say that a _____ is some kind of belief or claim that (supposedly) explains, asserts, or consolidates some class of claims. Additionally, in contrast with a theorem the statement of the _____ is generally accepted only in some tentative fashion as opposed to regarding it as having been conclusively established.

   a. Defined
   b. Theory
   c. Per mil
   d. Transport of structure

7. In mathematics, a _____ of an integer n is an integer which evenly divides n without leaving a remainder.

For example, 7 is a _____ of 42 because 42/7 = 6. We also say 42 is divisible by 7 or 42 is a multiple of 7 or 7 divides 42 or 7 is a factor of 42 and we usually write 7 | 42.

   a. 120-cell
   b. 1-center problem
   c. 2-3 heap
   d. Divisor

8. _____ is the self-government of a nation, country or some portion thereof, generally exercising sovereignty.

The term _____ is used in contrast to subjugation, which refers to a region as a 'territory' --subject to the political and military control of an external government. The word is sometimes used in a weaker sense to contrast with hegemony, the indirect control of one nation by another, more powerful nation.

   a. Independence
   b. A posteriori
   c. A Mathematical Theory of Communication
   d. A chemical equation

9. _____ is a special mathematical relationship between two quantities.Two quantities are called proportional if they vary in such a way that one of the quantities is a constant multiple of the other, or equivalently if they have a constant ratio.
   a. Depth
   b. Compression
   c. Discontinuity
   d. Proportionality

10. The _____ was the first of the apportionment paradoxes to be discovered. The US House of Representatives is Constitutionally required to allocate seats based on population counts, which are required every 10 years. The size of the House is set by statute.
   a. Infinity
   b. A Mathematical Theory of Communication
   c. Alabama paradox
   d. Implicit differentiation

11. In ring theory, a branch of abstract algebra, an _____ is a special subset of a ring. The _____ concept generalizes in an appropriate way some important properties of integers like 'even number' or 'multiple of 3'.

For instance, in rings one studies prime _____s instead of prime numbers, one defines coprime _____s as a generalization of coprime numbers, and one can prove a generalized Chinese remainder theorem about _____s.

   a. Element
   b. Equity
   c. Ideal
   d. Equaliser

Chapter 15. Graph Theory

1. In the study of metric spaces in mathematics, there are various notions of two metrics on the same underlying space being 'the same', or _____.

In the following, M will denote a non-empty set and d_1 and d_2 will denote two metrics on M.

The two metrics d_1 and d_2 are said to be topologically _____ if they generate the same topology on M.

   a. A posteriori
   b. A Mathematical Theory of Communication
   c. A chemical equation
   d. Equivalent

2. In graph theory, a _____ is an edge that connects a vertex to itself. A simple graph contains no _____s.

Depending on the context, a graph or a multigraph may be defined so as to either allow or disallow the presence of _____s:

   - Where graphs are defined so as to allow _____s and multiple edges, a graph without _____s is often called a multigraph.
   - Where graphs are defined so as to disallow _____s and multiple edges, a multigraph or a pseudograph is often defined to mean a 'graph' which can have _____s and multiple edges.

For an undirected graph, the degree of a vertex is equal to the number of adjacent vertices.

A special case is a _____, which adds two to the degree.

   a. Commensurable
   b. Duality
   c. FISH
   d. Loop

3. In mathematics, _____ and undefined are used to explain whether or not expressions have meaningful, sensible, and unambiguous values. Not all branches of mathematics come to the same conclusion.

The following expressions are undefined in all contexts, but remarks in the analysis section may apply.

   a. Plugging in
   b. Toy model
   c. LHS
   d. Defined

4. In graph theory, a _____ in a graph is a sequence of vertices such that from each of its vertices there is an edge to the next vertex in the sequence. The first vertex is called the start vertex and the last vertex is called the end vertex. Both of them are called end or terminal vertices of the _____.
   a. Class
   b. Blinding
   c. Deltoid
   d. Path

5. The word _____ has many distinct meanings in different fields of knowledge, depending on their methodologies and the context of discussion. Broadly speaking we can say that a _____ is some kind of belief or claim that (supposedly) explains, asserts, or consolidates some class of claims. Additionally, in contrast with a theorem the statement of the _____ is generally accepted only in some tentative fashion as opposed to regarding it as having been conclusively established.

a. Theory
b. Per mil
c. Transport of structure
d. Defined

6. In geometry, a _____ is a special kind of point, usually a corner of a polygon, polyhedron, or higher dimensional polytope. In the geometry of curves a _____ is a point of where the first derivative of curvature is zero. In graph theory, a _____ is the fundamental unit out of which graphs are formed
a. Dini
b. Duality
c. Crib
d. Vertex

7. A _____ is a structure built to span a gorge, valley, road, railroad track, river, body of water for the purpose of providing passage over the obstacle. Designs of _____s will vary depending on the function of the _____ and the nature of the terrain where the _____ is to be constructed. Roman _____ of Córdoba, Spain, built in the 1st century BC. Ponte di Pietra in Verona, Italy. A log _____ in the French Alps near Vallorcine. An English 18th century example of a _____ in the Palladian style, with shops on the span: Pulteney _____, Bath A Han Dynasty Chinese miniature model of two residential towers joined by a _____

The first _____s were made by nature -- as simple as a log fallen across a stream.

a. 2-3 heap
b. Bridge
c. 1-center problem
d. 120-cell

8. _____ is an adjective meaning contiguous, adjoining or abutting.

In geometry, _____ is when sides meet to make an angle.

In trigonometry the _____ side of a right angled triangle is the cathetus next to the angle in question.

a. Adjacent
b. Ambient space
c. Affine geometry
d. Ordered geometry

9. In graph theory, an _____ of a vertex v in a graph is a vertex that is connected to v by an edge. The neighbourhood of a vertex v in a graph G is the induced subgraph of G consisting of all vertices adjacent to v and all edges connecting two such vertices. For example, the image shows a graph of 6 vertices and 7 edges.
a. Articulation point
b. Induced path
c. Independent set
d. Adjacent vertex

10. In graph theory, an _____ is a path in a graph which visits each edge exactly once. Similarly, an Eulerian circuit is an _____ which starts and ends on the same vertex. They were first discussed by Leonhard Euler while solving the famous Seven Bridges of Königsberg problem in 1736.
a. Adjacent vertex
b. Isomorphism of graphs
c. Eulerian path
d. Independent set

11. In mathematics, a _____ is a statement that can be proved on the basis of explicitly stated or previously agreed assumptions.

a. Theorem
b. Disjunction introduction
c. Boolean function
d. Logical value

12. A _____ is a software program that facilitates symbolic mathematics. The core functionality of a CAS is manipulation of mathematical expressions in symbolic form.

The symbolic manipulations supported typically include

- simplification to the smallest possible expression or some standard form, including automatic simplification with assumptions and simplification with constraints
- substitution of symbolic, functors or numeric values for expressions
- change of form of expressions: expanding products and powers, partial and full factorization, rewriting as partial fractions, constraint satisfaction, rewriting trigonometric functions as exponentials, etc.
- partial and total differentiation
- symbolic constrained and unconstrained global optimization
- solution of linear and some non-linear equations over various domains
- solution of some differential and difference equations
- taking some limits
- some indefinite and definite integration, including multidimensional integrals
- integral transforms
- arbitrary-precision numeric operations
- Series operations such as expansion, summation and products
- matrix operations including products, inverses, etc.
- display of mathematical expressions in two-dimensional mathematical form, often using typesetting systems similar to TeX
- add-ons for use in applied mathematics such as physics packages for physical computation
- plotting graphs and parametric plots of functions in two and three dimensions, and animating them
- APIs for linking it on an external program such as a database, or using in a programming language to use the _____
- drawing charts and diagrams
- string manipulation such as matching and searching
- statistical computation
- Theorem proving and verification
- graphic production and editing such as CGI and signal processing as image processing
- sound synthesis

Many also include a programming language, allowing users to implement their own algorithms.

Some _____s focus on a specific area of application; these are typically developed in academia and are free.

a. 2-3 heap
b. 120-cell
c. 1-center problem
d. Computer algebra system

Chapter 15. Graph Theory

13. In mathematics, computing, linguistics and related subjects, an _____ is a sequence of finite instructions, often used for calculation and data processing. It is formally a type of effective method in which a list of well-defined instructions for completing a task will, when given an initial state, proceed through a well-defined series of successive states, eventually terminating in an end-state. The transition from one state to the next is not necessarily deterministic; some _____s, known as probabilistic _____s, incorporate randomness.

    a. In-place algorithm   b. Approximate counting algorithm
    c. Out-of-core   d. Algorithm

14. In mathematics, hyperbolic n-space, denoted H^n, is the maximally symmetric, simply connected, n-dimensional Riemannian manifold with constant sectional curvature −1. _____ is the principal example of a space exhibiting hyperbolic geometry. It can be thought of as the negative-curvature analogue of the n-sphere.

    a. Margulis lemma   b. Hyperbolic geometry
    c. Horocycle   d. Hyperbolic space

15. In mathematical analysis, a metric space M is said to be _____ (or Cauchy) if every Cauchy sequence of points in M has a limit that is also in M or alternatively if every Cauchy sequence in M converges in M.

Intuitively, a space is _____ if there are no 'points missing' from it (inside or at the boundary.) For instance, the set of rational numbers is not _____, because $\sqrt{2}$ is 'missing' from it, even though one can construct a Cauchy sequence of rational numbers that converges to it.

    a. 1-center problem   b. 2-3 heap
    c. 120-cell   d. Complete

16. In the mathematical field of graph theory, a _____ is a simple graph in which every pair of distinct vertices is connected by an edge. The _____ on n vertices has n vertices and n edges, and is denoted by K_n. It is a regular graph of degree n − 1.

    a. 120-cell   b. 1-center problem
    c. Wheel graph   d. Complete graph

17. _____ is a book by Matt Curtin about cryptography.

In this book, the author accounts his involvement in the DESCHALL Project, mobilizing thousands of personal computers in 1997 in order to meet the challenge to crack a single message encrypted with DES.

This was and remains one of the largest collaborations of any kind on a single project in history.

    a. Development   b. Blind
    c. Congruent   d. Brute Force

18. In set theory, a _____ is a partially ordered set such that for each $t \in T$, the set $\{s \in T : s < t\}$ is well-ordered by the relation <. For each $t \in T$, the order type of $\{s \in T : s < t\}$ is called the height of t. The height of T itself is the least ordinal greater than the height of each element of T.

    a. Definable numbers   b. Set-theoretic topology
    c. Transitive reduction   d. Tree

19. In the mathematical field of graph theory, a _____ T of a connected, undirected graph G is a tree composed of all the vertices and some of the edges of G. Informally, a _____ of G is a selection of edges of G that form a tree spanning every vertex. That is, every vertex lies in the tree, but no cycles are formed.

a. Germ
b. Lattice
c. Chord
d. Spanning tree

20. A _____ is a large fiber or metal rope, used for hauling, lifting or an assembly of two or more insulated electrical conductors, laid up together as an assembly. An optical _____ contains one or more optical fibers in a protective jacket that supports the fibers.

Ropes made of multiple strands of natural fibers such as hemp, sisal, manila, and cotton have been used for millennia for hoisting and hauling.

a. 2-3 heap
b. 1-center problem
c. 120-cell
d. Cable

ANSWER KEY

Chapter 1

1. b	2. b	3. d	4. d	5. b	6. c	7. a	8. d	9. d	10. b
11. d	12. d	13. d	14. b	15. d	16. d	17. b	18. b	19. d	20. b
21. b	22. b	23. b	24. d	25. c	26. b	27. d	28. b	29. d	30. b
31. a	32. a	33. d	34. a	35. b	36. a	37. c	38. d	39. d	40. b
41. b	42. a	43. d	44. a	45. d	46. d				

Chapter 2

1. b	2. d	3. b	4. a	5. d	6. d	7. a	8. d	9. a	10. d
11. d	12. b	13. d	14. c	15. c	16. d	17. a	18. d	19. d	20. b
21. d	22. a	23. a	24. d	25. a	26. d	27. b			

Chapter 3

1. a	2. b	3. b	4. d	5. a	6. d	7. d	8. a	9. a	10. a
11. c	12. d	13. c	14. d	15. c	16. d	17. b	18. a	19. a	20. d
21. b	22. d	23. b	24. b						

Chapter 4

1. a	2. d	3. a	4. c	5. d	6. b	7. d	8. a	9. d	10. d
11. a	12. d	13. a	14. d	15. d	16. d	17. d	18. d	19. a	20. d
21. a	22. a	23. d	24. b						

Chapter 5

1. b	2. d	3. d	4. a	5. b	6. d	7. d	8. d	9. b	10. c
11. d	12. b	13. d	14. d	15. d	16. c	17. d	18. d	19. d	20. d
21. c	22. d	23. c	24. d	25. d	26. d	27. d	28. d	29. a	30. d
31. d	32. a	33. c	34. c	35. d	36. d	37. c	38. b	39. d	40. c
41. b	42. d	43. d	44. d	45. d	46. d	47. d	48. b	49. c	50. d
51. d	52. d	53. d	54. d	55. d	56. b	57. d	58. d	59. d	60. d
61. b	62. c	63. d	64. c	65. d	66. d	67. d	68. b	69. d	70. d
71. d	72. d								

Chapter 6

1. d	2. d	3. a	4. d	5. b	6. d	7. c	8. d	9. c	10. a
11. a	12. d	13. d	14. d	15. a	16. d	17. d	18. a	19. d	20. d
21. b	22. d	23. c	24. b	25. d	26. d	27. d	28. b	29. d	30. d
31. b	32. b	33. b	34. d	35. d	36. d	37. b	38. d	39. b	40. d
41. a	42. b								

Chapter 7

1. d	2. a	3. c	4. b	5. c	6. b	7. b	8. b	9. b	10. d
11. d	12. b	13. d	14. b	15. d	16. b	17. d	18. a	19. b	20. a
21. d	22. c	23. b	24. c	25. a	26. d	27. c	28. d	29. b	30. d
31. d	32. c	33. d	34. c	35. d	36. d	37. d	38. b	39. b	40. d
41. d	42. b	43. a	44. b	45. b	46. c	47. d	48. b	49. c	50. d
51. d	52. b	53. d	54. b	55. d	56. b				

Chapter 8
1. a	2. d	3. d	4. c	5. d	6. b	7. d	8. d	9. d	10. d
11. d	12. c	13. c	14. c	15. a	16. d	17. a	18. d	19. d	20. b
21. a	22. c	23. d	24. d	25. a	26. d	27. d	28. d	29. b	30. d

Chapter 9
1. a	2. d	3. d	4. d	5. d	6. b	7. c	8. d	9. d	10. c
11. d	12. b	13. d	14. c	15. d	16. a	17. d			

Chapter 10
1. c	2. a	3. b	4. d	5. b	6. d	7. b	8. c	9. d	10. d
11. d	12. d	13. d	14. d	15. d	16. c	17. d	18. d	19. d	20. b
21. c	22. d	23. d	24. d	25. d	26. a	27. d	28. b	29. d	30. c
31. d	32. a	33. d	34. c	35. d	36. d	37. d	38. b	39. d	40. d
41. d	42. d	43. c	44. d	45. d	46. d	47. d	48. d	49. d	50. a
51. d	52. d	53. b	54. d	55. b	56. d	57. d	58. d	59. b	60. d
61. a	62. a	63. d	64. d	65. d	66. d	67. d	68. d	69. c	70. d
71. d	72. b	73. a	74. d	75. d	76. c	77. a	78. c	79. b	80. d
81. a	82. d	83. a	84. c	85. d	86. c	87. b	88. a	89. a	90. a
91. c	92. d	93. d	94. c	95. a	96. d	97. d	98. b	99. d	100. d
101. d	102. c	103. b	104. d	105. c	106. d	107. d	108. b		

Chapter 11
1. c	2. b	3. d	4. d	5. d	6. d	7. d	8. c	9. d	10. d
11. d	12. d	13. a	14. d	15. d	16. d	17. c	18. d	19. c	20. d
21. c	22. d	23. c	24. b	25. d	26. d	27. d	28. d	29. d	30. c
31. b	32. d	33. d	34. a	35. a					

Chapter 12
1. a	2. d	3. d	4. b	5. d	6. d	7. a	8. b	9. a	10. d
11. d	12. b	13. c	14. a	15. b	16. a	17. d	18. d	19. d	20. c
21. c	22. d	23. d	24. d	25. c	26. a	27. a	28. b	29. b	30. a
31. b	32. c	33. b	34. d	35. d	36. a	37. c	38. d	39. c	40. b
41. b	42. c	43. a	44. d	45. d	46. b	47. c	48. a	49. d	50. b
51. d	52. c	53. d	54. d	55. d	56. d	57. c	58. d	59. b	60. c

Chapter 13
1. a	2. d	3. d	4. b	5. c	6. c	7. c	8. d	9. d	10. c
11. d	12. d	13. a	14. a	15. c	16. d	17. d	18. c	19. c	20. d
21. c	22. b	23. b	24. d	25. c	26. d	27. c	28. d	29. d	

Chapter 14
1. b	2. d	3. a	4. b	5. c	6. b	7. d	8. a	9. d	10. c
11. c									

ANSWER KEY

Chapter 15

1. d	2. d	3. d	4. d	5. a	6. d	7. b	8. a	9. d	10. c
11. a	12. d	13. d	14. d	15. d	16. d	17. d	18. d	19. d	20. d

www.ingramcontent.com/pod-product-compliance
Lightning Source LLC
Chambersburg PA
CBHW082046230426
43670CB00016B/2790